JOHN GIERACH

At the Grave of the Unknown Fisherman

Illustrated by Glenn Wolff

SIMON & SCHUSTER

NEW YORK   LONDON   TORONTO   SYDNEY   SINGAPORE

SIMON & SCHUSTER
Rockefeller Center
1230 Avenue of the Americas
New York, NY 10020

Copyright © 2003 by John Gierach

SIMON & SCHUSTER and colophon are registered trademarks
of Simon & Schuster, Inc.

For information about special discounts for bulk purchases,
please contact Simon & Schuster Special Sales:
1-800-456-6798 or business@simonandschuster.com

Illustrations © by Glenn Wolff

Manufactured in the United States of America

10   9   8   7   6   5   4   3

Portions of this book, in different form, first appeared in *Fly Rod and Reel, Gray's Sporting Journal,*
and *The Redstone Review.*

Library of Congress Cataloging-in-Publication Data
Gierach, John, 1946–
At the grave of the unknown fisherman / John Gierach.
p.   cm.
1. Fly fishing—Anecdotes. 2. Gierach, John, 1946– I. Title.
SH456.G545 2003
799.1'24—dc21   2002036541
ISBN 0-7432-2992-4

"I was awfully happy, not because life was so good, but because it was my life, and I was in it."

—SCOTT SPENCER

Chapter 1

By the calendar at least, it was early spring instead of late winter, although in the Rocky Mountain west that really *is* just a technical distinction, since one can be about as raw and unfriendly as the other. Four seasons have never been enough to adequately describe the weather here or anywhere else, for that matter. There should be at least a dozen, and they should designate the unstable edges where one set of conditions shade into the next, because those are the most interesting. The whole idea of seasons would be more useful if they'd been named by fishermen instead of astronomers.

Anyway, it was just before the last big snowstorms that come before mud season, and some friends and I were in Wyoming fishing some prairie lakes on a ranch the size of a small New Hampshire county. It was still too early in the season for these lakes to fish well (they're said not to really turn on until sometime in May), but this was when the invitation came, so this is when we went.

Too early or not, I was ready. It had been a long winter—fishingwise and otherwise. The big snowfalls in the mountains came late that year and the snowpack was high. The cozy romance of daily fires in the wood stoves at home had begun to lose some of its charm, and the scattered, almost warm days we'd had only meant that the local streams would soon be swollen with the runoff from all that snow and unfishable until late June.

Of course, a writer needs big chunks of time for work, and a fishing writer desperately needs for the fishing season to end—at least for a while. The season never does officially end here, but it ends effectively, which means you can fish if you want to and if you can stand it, but you don't *have* to.

I enjoy the writing as much as I do the fishing, so at first winter is almost a relief. By November it's clear that there won't be any good fishing to speak of for five months, and at the moment that seems like soon enough. It's not that I'm tired, just "well fished" as a friend says, and now it's time to sit back and practice my other skill: the one that pays the mortgage and lets me fish for the other seven months a year.

So when winter first comes, I'm all for it, but toward the end I'll find that in my off time I've been doing things like idly studying the properties of firewood. I can tell you that silver poplar burns well but too fast. Oak is slow, hot and businesslike, good for cooking and cold nights but not too exciting. Maple and walnut are close seconds to oak, and sometimes while splitting wood I'll find a walnut burl that's so intricate and pretty that I'll give it to a rod maker friend for reel seats instead of burning it. Osage orange is hard to get, but it's dense, muscular, heavy as coal, and relentless, so it's good for banking and damping down. Cottonwood is a signature tree of the west and one of my favorites, but it doesn't like to be used for firewood, so it pouts and stinks and puts out little heat. Pine isn't rated high as fuel, but I like it because it snaps and roars and seems to generate heat out of pure enthusiasm. I use pine on days when I want a happy fire.

I can also say that wood split by hand seems clean and orderly because with a wedge and maul you have to find the spot where a log wants to split, not where *you* want it to split. Wood from a mechanical splitter looks more torn and broken—sort of like wreckage—and, as a practical matter, it has more splinters.

Contemplating firewood is an interesting enough way to while away some time, but it may also be a sign that winter has ground on a little too long. That's how some winters can go. Before this one was over, the season had begun to seem like a preview of mortality, and I got the shack nasties so bad I just barely avoided ice fishing.

There were five of us in Wyoming that week: me, Mike Price, his friend Cliff Rice, and Bob and Mary Smith, fishing guides out of Saratoga who had access to the ranch. The first morning was dark and chilly and could have passed for November. During the height of fishing season, the little town of Saratoga bustles, but that week the place had a Sunday morning vacancy about it. Nothing much seemed to be going on, and it felt odd to be busy. We stowed our gear in a Suburban, and then Bob went out back to trailer up a couple of all-terrain vehicles he said we'd probably need. No one had been in to the lakes yet that year, but he was guessing that the last few miles in to some of them would be close to impassable.

The ATVs seemed like overkill, but I grasped the problem when we pulled off the paved road and started up onto the first bench of land on the ranch. The way the weather had been, these clay tracks would turn from dirty ice to slush to outright mud during what passed for the warmth of the day, and then slowly turn back again in the afternoon. At the moment they were ankle-deep and slimy under a delicately transparent sheen of brown ice that crackled under the tires. The trailer fishtailed. Things were starting to look expeditionary. It was clearly too early for real, paying clients.

Novelist Annie Proulx once described the Wyoming high plains as "dangerous and indifferent ground," but I've always liked them in spite of that—or maybe because of it. There's pine and juniper on the slopes of the foothills under the bare rim rock, petering out as you come down from the high ridges, and patches of cottonwood in the few places where there's water and shelter from the wind, but in the open everything is low, tough, scrubby, and sparse—sage and rabbitbrush, cactus and short grass. There's always a direction you can look that lets you see forever, and even when you can't spot them, you always have the feeling you're being watched by antelope.

It was cold and gray that week, and everything looked half-dead, with crusty old snow clinging in sculptured patches where the wind hadn't quite scoured it away yet. It probably wasn't dangerous—just chilly and windy—but it *did* seem indifferent. We were all happy to be there. I like to think of this country at this time of year as a paradise that not just anyone can recognize.

I rode in to the first lake perched on the back of an ATV. (I refuse to drive anything that doesn't have a steering wheel and a windshield.) We were on a winding, two-track Jeep trail that was muddy in some places, snowy in others, and badly rutted. Within fifty yards my back was plastered with mud from my hat to my butt, and it seemed to me that we were going too fast, but I held on and didn't say anything, while Bob and Mary's young black Lab Sonny ran ahead to make sure there were no gophers or jackrabbits in the way. If you don't give a dog a specific job, he'll improvise one for himself and it will invariably be fun. There's a lesson there.

The first lake was small—maybe five or six acres—and not really a lake at all, but a homemade, spring-fed reservoir for watering stock. It was down in a gentle swale but otherwise in the open with nothing to block the steady thirty-mile-an-hour wind. Springs run thin in the winter, so the water was down and there was a ring of mud around the shore. An ice shelf was still clinging to the southwest bank, and the water was distinctly brown, with beige foam lines churned up by wave action. The grass on the bank was still matted from a winter under snow, and it was the same shade of brown as the water and the mud. The whole place seemed weirdly monochromatic, like a sepia-tone photograph from the 1800s. Bob said there were brook trout there. Cliff added that they were "good ones."

These rich prairie lakes are spooky to fish even in the best conditions. They're known to grow large, healthy trout because of their water chemistry and the tremendous amount of food they produce, but precisely because there's so much to eat, the fish are often lazy and moody. As a friend once said of another freshwater shrimp–infested prairie lake, "All a trout has to do to get something to eat here is open his mouth."

Sometimes there will be something like a midge, mayfly, or damselfly hatch and the trout will show themselves at the surface, but more often they'll be cruising aimlessly at varying depths, eating this and that as it comes along. The lakes are more or less featureless: odd-shaped bowls with creases between the inlet and the dam marking the old creek channel. Until you can puzzle out the fine points—which can take as long as a season—one spot can seem about as promising as another.

We did the usual thing: We tied on heavily weighted streamers (each picking our own favorite patterns) and worked the water off what we thought were the steepest banks. You couldn't see more than a few inches into the brown water, but it just seemed like the kind of day when trout would swim deep.

I chose a spot for no other reason than wind direction—I wanted it blowing on my left shoulder to keep my right-handed cast away from my head—and tied on a trim, black Woolly Bugger with lead eyeballs. That's what I always start with when I'm standing on the shore of a new lake without a clue. I carry a lot of flies, but if that one doesn't work, I don't have a standard second choice. Some days you think you know what you're doing, even on new water. Other days you have to start at the beginning, as if you were the first fisherman.

I fished the Bugger slow and deep: long cast, long sink, then a crawling, halting retrieve, watching for live tics in the tip of the floating line as it bobbed in the chop. The strikes were light and easy to miss: little dead-feeling bumps that could just as easily have been the fly brushing a weed. In fact, most of them were just that. Four out of five suspected strikes brought back vegetation. That's annoying, but it does tell you you're fishing deep enough.

When I finally did set up on a fish, the fight was dogged and impressive—not a huge trout, but heavy and nowhere near ready to give up. It turned out to be a sixteen-inch brookie as square and solid as a brick, with a small head, a humped back, and a deep gut. He was well fed but still hungry enough to pick up a two-inch-long Bugger just to see if it was edible.

It was a fat, healthy fish, but it also looked washed out: silvery olive and pink where a brook trout is usually green and orange, with a hint of maroon on the tail, faint wormy lines on the dorsal and spots so pale you could just barely tell they were supposed to be yellow. At first glance it could have been a lake trout, an arctic char or a splake. I had to study it for a minute before deciding that, yes, this is indeed a brook trout.

During a break Bob said these fish brightened up some by fall, but that they never got really brilliant like those picture-book brook trout from Maine and Labrador. And why should they? One of the neatest things about fish is how they reflect their surroundings perfectly and effortlessly.

I may have been a little disappointed by them at first—or maybe just surprised because they weren't quite what I expected—but then I started thinking they were sort of pretty in a quiet, understated way. I even had a flashback to a perpetually muddy farm pond I used to fish where the big, fat bluegills were that same silvery pink. I remembered being momentarily confused by the first one, thinking it was a white crappie until I noticed the dark gill flap. I learned to like them, too, but then I guess it's always been easy for me to like fish.

We spent the afternoon catching brook trout that were between fourteen and seventeen inches, but with different builds so they were all about the same weight. Some of the longer fish were well proportioned, but the short ones were growing so fast in that rich pond that they'd put on more gut than length and seemed almost deformed. These things had been stocked as fingerlings a few years before and they were growing up nicely. In two more seasons they'd be hogs.

Eventually my hands started to sting from releasing fish in the cold water, so I put on the fingerless wool gloves. Not long after that I put the rain slicker on over the wool sweater to cut the chill of the wind, hoping it didn't get any colder because that was the end of the warm clothes.

In the next few days we fished some other lakes that had all been stocked with rainbows. For an hour or so back at the brookie lake,

Cliff and Mary had stood on a high, grassy bank and caught trout after trout casting out over the ice shelf, but for the most part the fishing was slow. We'd wander the shores of the different lakes, chucking streamers or nymphs, covering water, and now and then someone would hook a fish. Still, we caught trout everywhere we went. Even the smallest were respectable, and some were nice and big.

Sonny the dog was mildly interested in the fish, but he was more concerned with small mammals. Sometimes you could see him coursing through the sage in the distance, carefully adjusting his speed so he never quite caught whatever he was chasing. He always managed to join us for lunch, though. As oblivious as he sometimes seemed, he could apparently hear the crinkle of a sandwich wrapper at a hundred yards. The first day I thought he was the most skillful beggar I'd ever seen because he got a whole sandwich by just sitting down in front of Mary and grinning, but as it turned out it was his sandwich and he knew it. Mary explained that he didn't like to eat dog food when everyone else had ham and cheese. That seemed entirely reasonable, but then I've always been one to spoil animals. When Sonny was done with his own sandwich, he asked for part of mine and got it. This was a young dog who spent the better part of every day running. There wasn't an ounce of fat on him.

Sometimes the wind was so strong it was a small victory just to make a decent cast without hooking yourself, and when it was a long time between strikes you could almost begin to wonder if it was worth the trouble. Almost, but not quite. Lots of things occur to you while you're in the fisherman's trance, but the day you actually begin to wonder why you do this is the day you might as well sell your tackle and buy a bigger TV.

Eventually the Wyoming wind becomes a fact of life, as if it has blown forever and always will. I got one of my biggest rainbows on a crawdad pattern fished right on the bottom and the wind was blowing so hard I didn't even have to strip the thing in. The line blowing across the surface gave it all the action it needed.

Things always seemed on the verge of being out of control in that wind. There was the constant temptation to duck on the forward cast, because you knew your fly was coming forward, but you never knew quite from which direction and you were half-afraid to look. We were all doing it. There'd be the quick, low back cast, then the forward cast with a haul to get the line speed up, followed by a curt little bow. Beyond that, everyone seemed lost in their own thoughts.

Most of the rainbows were also a little on the pale side—like they'd been laundered too many times or left out in the sun too long—but by then it seemed fine. We were fishing at the wrong time, getting some anyway, and this was just how they looked. Like us, trout adjust themselves to where and how they live. The only difference is, trout almost always come out of it looking good. I've been on trips at other unlikely times of the year when I've suffered more and caught less—sometimes nothing at all—so when I'm getting them every day and some of them are nice and big, I guess they could be transparent for all I care.

We went in to all the lakes except one on the ATVs, and one day, when Cliff almost bucked me off for the fifth time, I finally pounded him on the back and yelled, "Slow down, damn it!" Which he did momentarily. I understood the idea of staying in motion so we wouldn't bog down, but I didn't think we needed to get air. When we stopped I apologized, but Cliff just grinned and said it was okay, pleased that he'd gone fast enough to scare me.

Cliff knew these lakes well, and that afternoon, after hauling a few big rainbows from a small lake, he started to go on about how it would be later in the year. It would be the calm early evening of a hot summer day with the light beginning to slant and the air just beginning to feel soft and cool. Trout would be rising to a hatch of #16 Speckled Duns; there would be deceptively delicate dimples and subsurface boils that would move a gallon of water. The fish wouldn't be pushovers, but if you kept at it you'd get some strikes. The grass would be lush, the cattails green and full of red-winged blackbirds, the sky blue, the white clouds turning pink, the ante-lope fat, songbirds singing, hawks circling, the air smelling of rab-bitbrush in bloom (like honey and wax).

Well, maybe he actually said all that and maybe I filled in some blanks for myself. I'd never seen it right there before, but I'd seen it plenty of other places. The first summer fishing in these high plains and low foothills is beautiful when it finally happens, but we were standing there on a crust of snow, bundled to the chin, and blowing on our fingers, and it still seemed a long way off.

At the end of each day we'd hose the worst of the mud from our waders and someone would make one of those inevitable comments like, "If you were gettin' twenty dollars an hour to work in these conditions, you'd quit." The rest of us would chuckle politely, agreeing that we must all be crazy. Nothing makes a fisherman happier than to have just proved that he must be crazy.

Okay, maybe I'm being overly dramatic in retrospect. It probably wasn't actually miserable, just the kind of happy struggle that sport can lure you into. There were times I wished the sun would come out and it would warm up and the wind would die, but I never wished I was back home watching television. (For that matter, there's a kind of Nordic, Protestant sense in which being too cold feels good.) Still, at the end of the day it was a relief to take hot showers, eat hot food in a nearly empty bar in town, and go back to a warm, dry room. After a few days it was even a little bit of a relief for Mike and me to finally pack up my truck and begin the drive back to Colorado.

I've always been a little bit of a foul-weather fisherman, although some days I think I enjoy having *done* it more than actually doing it. It could be I'm out to prove something, or greedily stretch the season, or avoid the regret that can come from staying comfortably at home. But more likely it's just the result of an unconscious decision made a lifetime ago; the one where catching a few pale fish in a pale landscape a month before anyone else even gets on the water is an unquestionably worthwhile thing to do.

Years ago, when I was a wild teenager still unsure of the difference between self-destruction and just playing hard, my dad told me it didn't make sense to beat yourself over the head just because it felt good when you stopped—although of course it *did* feel good. He thought I was just going through a phase, but if I was, it's been a damned long one.

Mike and I drove out to the highway and stopped at a roadhouse where we bought two cups of coffee so oily and bitter we'd have poured them out in the parking lot if it hadn't been so far to the next joint. Then we settled in for the five-hour drive home. We were in clean, dry clothes, the heater was going, and we were talking about fishing. It was just barely spring, but it was spring nonetheless, and we had the whole season ahead of us.

CHAPTER 2

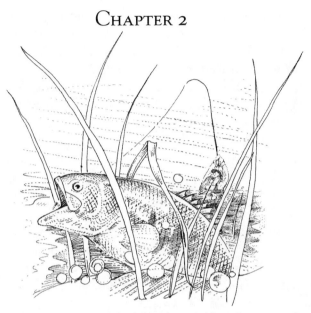

A month later I was fishing in the wind again—or trying to. This time it was warmer but stronger—making casting impossible instead of just difficult—and it had been howling for three days straight. We'd tried to fish a few times—looking for sheltered, tree-lined banks where we could cast deer-hair bugs, or trolling big rabbit fur streamers out in the open water—but we hadn't hooked a bass in recent memory, and it had begun to look pointless. Then the battery on my trolling motor went dead because my charger wasn't working right, so we rowed the john boat in—half a mile, against a strong headwind—and retired to our rented cabin to wait it out.

The good news about the cabin was that it was dirt cheap: twenty-four dollars a day, split two ways. The bad news was, it used to be a chicken coop, so it was tiny, and my partner Ed Engle, at six feet some inches, couldn't stand up straight in it without bumping his head, which he did every half hour or so, on average. It pissed him off at first, but he finally seemed to accept it as the price you pay for being a tall man staying in a short, cheap shack. This was your basic shelter, stove, and a dry bed, but it wasn't the kind of place where you're meant to spend much time.

Ed and I have fished for a long time, and we've both worked regular jobs outside, so we know about waiting out weather. We know about the tendency to jabber for an hour about something that normally wouldn't be worth more than a passing comment; to argue about things neither of us really care about; and to laugh insanely at things that aren't particularly funny. We know about all that, but we succumb to it anyway.

On the other hand, we agree that if you have to be weather-bound in a claustrophobic fishing cabin, it's best to do it with an old friend: someone with whom you have thirty years' worth of shared stories that you both think should be aired out from time to time. We dredged up a lot of our collective pasts—usually in short, furious, caffeine-induced fits—and some of it was all but unrecognizable now in the retelling. When we got tired of that, we read novels, drank more coffee as the buzz faded, and now and then went out to stand leaning into the howling wind and shout, "I think it's starting to die down a little!"

We're both avid readers, and on long trips we each travel with what amount to small libraries for just these kinds of situations. (A free day to read a book isn't all bad, although on a fishing trip it's not all good either.) But eventually we'd decide to drive around to some of the lakes, just to look at birds and break up the monotony. Since the john boat was always strapped to the top of the pickup anyway, we'd usually end up trying to fish a little, even though it was useless and possibly dangerous to be on the water. If one of us caught a bass or even a small pike, it all seemed worthwhile. If not, at least the struggle killed some time.

This is fishing. It's how we have decided we want to spend our lives.

The trip had actually started out well enough. On the first day we'd pulled in at about four in the afternoon after a seven-hour drive from home and launched the boat on the nearest lake. We fished some flooded timber along the east shore for a few hours, landed five good-sized bass between us, and I missed one that was so big he scared me and I set the hook too soon. I wrote it off to road burn.

That night, as we were talking about all the places we wanted to fish while we were there, the wind picked up. It was just a little *whoosh* at first, but then trees started to lean and windows rattled. As I think I mentioned, it blew hard for the next three days without so much as stopping to take a breath.

We agreed that it couldn't blow forever, although in that country at that time of year it could certainly blow for a couple of weeks straight. We talked about our previous spring trips out here to the northern plains; about how we'd suffered in and waited through crappy weather of every description and finally had those few days when we hammered big fish. It must eventually work out in the end or we wouldn't keep coming back. I mean, we're not stupid—are we?

We've been going to this same place for several years now, ever since Ed sniffed it out by doggedly following up some vague rumors, and it's beginning to shape up as one of those necessary high points in any fishing season: something we'll continue to do every spring unless there's a good reason not to.

The place is profoundly rural. It's a two-hour drive from the nearest town of any size. It's peaceful, uncrowded, largely unimproved, lousy with wildlife (including ticks), and the fishing is good but not *too* good. This is the kind of spot that slips nicely between the cracks. The fishing is well above average, but it's not fabulous enough to attract the headhunters; and it's a white-bread, wieners, and pork and beans kind of place that will never be frequented by the big-ticket types, either. This is the regional, low-rent resort area that some of us grew up with in the Midwest and that still flourishes here and there around the country, except instead of "flourishing" they'd be more likely to say they're "gettin' by."

There's a generous handful of shallow, weedy lakes scattered around in over seventy thousand acres of sprawling sandhills and prairie marsh country that's in turn surrounded by ranch and farm territory. All the lakes have largemouth bass and bluegills, most have northern pike, some have saugeye (a kind of designer walleye), and one lake holds muskies. A few of the lakes are within sight of paved county roads, but others are a long grind down winding dirt tracks where you travel at speeds that don't register on the speedometer and where you have to stop often to move turtles out of your way. (Only a heartless swine would knowingly squash a turtle.)

You'll see other fishermen, but never so many that there isn't plenty of water to fish. They're in a variety of craft, from the occasional uptown bass boat with swivel seats and warp-drive trolling motors fore and aft, to the equally occasional small canoe dangerously overloaded with large men and industrial-sized coolers, but most are in modest, sensible fishing boats.

What they call "boat ramps" are basically dirt roads that end abruptly in the water, and these are where you have most of your conversations with other fishermen: short ones when you're going out in the morning, longer, more relaxed ones when you're coming back in.

The trolling motor on my john boat is a recent development. We use it to get around on the big lakes, but we rarely actually troll with it. For the first few years we were completely hand-powered, with just oars and a twelve-foot spruce pole for pushing our way back into the tules to fish the hidden potholes that most people leave alone.

One guy called it "Louisiana fishin'" and said he hadn't seen it done in years, but some other fishermen were a little weirded out that we were non-motorized. One day, as we were putting in at one of the lakes, a man seemed puzzled that we were so low-tech.

He strolled over with his hands in his pockets, watched us haul the boat down to the water, and then said, "No motor?"

"Nope."

"No motor at all?"

"No motor."

"Just oars?"

"Yup, oars and a pole."

"Really?"

"Really."

"Well, okay then."

A day later, the battery on that guy's trolling motor went dead and he and his canoe had to be towed off the lake because he didn't have a paddle. We didn't say anything. Didn't have to.

The place is uncrowded enough that you'll usually have a boat ramp to yourself, but there are also enough people around that if you wait for a while, someone will show up. The year before there'd been two old, frail-looking guys in a 1960-something pickup towing an ancient boat and trailer. We saw them often because they liked the same lakes we did. They'd pull up to a boat launch and stand around drinking coffee until someone stopped and said, "You two need some help?" Then one of them would glance at his coffee cup as if he'd just noticed he was holding it and say, "Yup."

Same thing when they came off the lake, usually with a modest stringer of fish for supper. They'd beach the boat and stand around until someone said, "Need a hand there?"

"Well, it wouldn't hurt."

They say the best time to fish these Midwestern prairie lakes is in the spring when the weeds are still down. These are shallow, seep lakes with lots of common reeds, bulrushes, and lily pads: leathery, deeply rooted, fly-grabbing, fish-tangling aquatic plants. Even early in the season the fishing can be sticky, with difficult casting and many fish lost to snags. When you hook a bass in this thick stuff, there's a green and silver flash, and you set up and haul hard, not giving an inch. The man on the pole pushes forward and you lip lock the fish in mid-fight. You get him—and that's the whole idea—but it's over too soon, as if you'd just finished the best book you ever read and wish it had gone on for another fifty pages.

Then again, most of the fishermen who tell you how hard it is once the weeds are up are going after pike with hardware and spinning tackle. Some of these people are very good at what they do, but I think when you're fishing for bass with floating bugs and a fly rod, you have a little more leeway with the weed cover. That's how Ed and I approach it. We spend a lot of time working the densest cover where the spin fishers don't go and we often do well.

But it can be good for a fly caster to spend some time around spin fishermen. The older ones especially remind me of the men many of us grew up with: the dads, uncles, and other assorted guys in baseball caps who were handy around motors, prone to laughter, and generous with kids and strangers. They're a little more likely than your average fly caster to legally kill and eat some fish, but a little *less* likely to be deadly serious about it.

Sometimes we do some wade fishing or belly boating on the one small lake you have to hike in to, but mostly we fish from a boat here like everyone else, so there's all that marginally nautical stuff to fool with. That also reminds Ed and me of our childhoods when, we now think, fishing was quieter, more casual, less hurried, and generally better. Maybe it really was, or maybe that's just something you start to imagine as you get older.

The little fish camp we stay at is also sort of nostalgic, with its cheap, down-at-the-heels cabins, fish-cleaning shack, and the office/bait shop/general store where the lady behind the counter always has the current weather report and the latest rumors, plus the regulation bulletin board with Polaroids of people holding large dead fish.

This is also one of those regular trips that tend to breed the minor catastrophes that make for a real adventure. In years past we've gotten frozen out in cold weather, pounded by rain and hail, been issued speeding tickets by cops who came out of nowhere in places where you think you can see for fifty miles in any direction, and gotten hopelessly stuck in the mud at boat ramps.

I remember being stuck to the axles on a cold, rainy day at a lake we'd never tried before. There was no one else on the lake, and we hadn't seen another car on the road in, but not five minutes later two men in a big V-8 pickup towing a serious bass boat pulled up. The driver rolled down his window and asked, "You got a chain?"

"Yeah," I said.

He said, "Well, let's do 'er, then."

He pulled us out easily, and as I drove up to some firm ground to park, the transmission started making an ugly groaning noise. Ed said, "I don't think it's supposed to sound like that."

A week before, back home, I'd faced that old dilemma: the one where you can afford to fix the clutch or go fishing but—clutches being what they are—probably not both. But then my neighbor-hood truck guru said, "Aw hell, drive it till it breaks and *then* fix it," which sounded like good advice until it started making bad sounds out on the Great Plains, forty miles from the nearest mechanic.

We carried the boat down to the water and fished in the rain for a few hours, getting halfhearted bumps from the baby pike they call "hammer handles," until we were finally driven off by wind and cold. We ate lunch in the truck with the heater blasting and the wipers going so we could watch the geese flying under the low ceiling. The conversation had gotten as far as old girlfriends and dead fishing buddies when Ed said, "Well, I'm a student of luck, and I say before it's all over one of us is gonna catch a great big fish."

I remember thinking, I don't care, I just love being out here. And maybe that was it—some kind of Zen thing about letting go of desire—because a few hours later on a different lake I caught a bass we guessed at six or seven pounds. He ate a red and yellow Bunny Leech cast up into some bulrushes where I thought maybe I'd get a pike.

I guess it would be a better story if the fish weighed twice that much, but six pounds is real good for that water, and I've learned that the trick to being a happy fisherman is to be easily pleased.

The trip went on from there. More fish were caught—mostly pike—the weather stayed wet and bitter, there were long talks, long silences, second and third cups of coffee on rainy mornings, and the delicious drama of whether or not the truck would break down, and if so, where.

Of course, I couldn't have known it then, but the clutch would last another three months, finally to die quietly at home, among friends.

• • •

On this last trip, we had wind, rain, lightning, a little hail, an early-season tornado that missed us by a good twenty miles one night but still nearly blew the cabin down, and a leak in the truck's cooling system that we managed to fix temporarily with a sharpened stick, some electrical tape, and a jug of lake water. And I wrenched my back one day when I came within inches of stepping on a three-foot-long bull snake.

It was the good old American heartland, where everything is incomparably beautiful as long as it's not so windy you can't stand, so wet your house floats, so cold it freezes your eyeballs, or so hot the sky feels like an anvil on your head. This is where I grew up. It's also why I moved away.

It wasn't too far from here that, years ago now, I went into a public toilet and found a sign that said, IF YOU DON'T THROW YOUR CIGARETTE BUTTS IN OUR URINALS, WE WON'T PEE IN YOUR ASH-TRAYS. Ten years later, in the same facility, the sign had changed to, ATTENTION HIPPIES: PLEASE DON'T EAT THE URINAL CAKES. Things were changing, but in the heartland the response was still the old fatalism peppered with humor, and it still seemed to work. I mean, if you were a hippie walking out of the toilet, someone would likely give you a big, shit-eating grin—possibly the same guy who put up the sign. You couldn't help but grin back, and that was the end of it. The only way you could get into trouble was if you couldn't take a joke.

Once, back in the 1960s, I was sitting at a kitchen table with my Aunt Dora, Uncle Leonard, and some assorted cousins. I wore a long beard and hair down to my shoulders then, and although that didn't really seem to bother anyone, I can't say no one took notice of it.

I'd been traveling a lot out west and was passing around some snapshots. One showed me standing above tree line in an old canvas hunting coat, holding the collar of a large, rabid-looking husky with one ear missing. Stretched out behind me was the gorgeous snowcapped spine of the Continental Divide. Aunt Dora asked, innocently, "How high were you here?" There was a long, embarrassed silence, and then Uncle Leonard said, "I think she's talkin' about altitude."

It wasn't far from that kitchen where I'd caught my first fish at age four or five and immediately learned to love fishing. It was also here that I got the idea that fishermen were people who spent so much time neglecting more important things that they eventually redefined importance, and who probably had more fun than they had a right to. That sounded okay to me then, and still does.

That's why I still love the Midwest and can still feel at home there for as much as a week at a time, even though I now live far away from it and wouldn't have it any other way. But as someone once said, when you're really *from* a place, you never get over it. For instance, whenever I'm back in that country, I feel an urge to write things on the walls of public toilets—official-sounding notices that begin, ATTENTION REDNECKS. . . . So far I've always been able to stop myself, but the impulse remains after thirty years.

We native Midwesterners also think we share a kind of inherited wisdom. We know that life is hard and that, although virtue isn't usually rewarded, it is still somehow its own reward. We know about the American Dream, too: not the one you hear about now where you get fabulously wealthy overnight through dumb luck and then turn into an asshole, but the one where you work hard, stay honest, don't complain too much, get in some fishing, and end up doing okay. We also understand that the movie *Fargo* was not a comedy.

So the wind continued to blow, and we continued to wait it out. Every evening we'd go over and check the gut bucket at the fish-cleaning shed to see if anyone else was doing any good. Sometimes there'd be the remains of a few little bullheads or a lonesome saug-eye, but usually it was empty and that made us feel better. Skunked fishermen love company.

But then the early morning of the fourth day was only breezy, and after all that high wind it felt eerie, the way they say it does in the eye of a hurricane. So we bolted breakfast and raised a cloud of dust heading for the lake we'd agreed to fish as soon as we could get out. (You'd think that after all that wind there wouldn't be any dust left, but apparently there's an endless supply.) It was the small lake we'd have to hike in to, so it would be float tubes instead of the relative comfort of the john boat, but the lake was sheltered by high bluffs and known for its bullfrogs and fat bass.

The breeze had picked up a bit by the time we'd driven out there, walked in, and were rigged to fish, but it still seemed manageable— at least by comparison—so I paddled out to some offshore weeds and Ed made for some flooded timber farther up the shore.

I'd already tied on the garishly colored deer-hair diving frog that's become my favorite bass pattern, and I started picking up fish right away. I was casting to the edges of the weed bed, to the open potholes, and right into the weeds themselves in places where they were thin enough to let the fly hit the water. I'd swim the bug if there was enough room; otherwise I'd just let it sit, but the fish were hungry, so it didn't seem to matter what I did.

The smaller bass exploded on the fly, throwing spray in the air, but the bigger ones took with a quiet, almost troutlike slurp, having learned not to work any harder than necessary. I lost a few to the tough weeds, but I landed most of them by keeping the rod high and hauling hard. I was fishing an old Heddon bamboo rod, a 6½-ounce, 9-foot, 9-weight built for heavy work back in the days before finesse became fashionable.

Ed was a hundred yards away casting into the bleached, flooded timber. Every second or third time I looked over there his rod was bent. I guessed this was it: the one day (at least) that this trip always grudgingly gives up and that always seems like enough.

The wind must have picked up gradually, because I didn't really notice it until the waves had turned to whitecaps that loudly slapped the side of the tube and threw a fine spray in my face. I might not have noticed even then, except that the bass had also stopped biting.

Ed and I paddled in and took a break on shore, sitting with our backs to the wind and using our belly boats as easy chairs. The wind was up pretty seriously by then, and we'd both caught quite a few good bass, but we didn't even think about going back to the cabin. I don't think either of us could face it.

The wind was too strong to go back out in the tubes, so we decided to fish the weedy slough on our side of the lake, thinking maybe some fish would be lying in the weeds to get out of the chop.

Ed and I headed off in opposite directions and were each fishing alone, but we both figured it out pretty quickly. There were bass lying motionless here and there in the thick tules and rushes, sometimes with the tips of their dorsal fins breaking the surface in water as shallow as six inches. We flushed the first few, then picked up on it and started looking for them, hunting along like herons.

There were also schools of big bullfrog tadpoles milling around in loose pods: hundreds of them, some already starting to sprout legs. It made perfect sense. A bullfrog tadpole is a full three inches long: big, round, and juicy. A small handful of them would stuff a five-pound bass to the gills and even just one would be worth a long stalk.

I left on my deer-hair diving frog because it was roughly the right size and shape to be a tadpole, never mind the color. The tadpoles themselves were a sort of dull greenish slate, while the bass bug was chartreuse, orange, yellow, and black with pink and green rubber legs. But that's not the kind of thing that bothers a hungry bass—God bless 'em.

Between the wind and the thick weeds, it was difficult casting, and the bass were hard to spot, but when I could get the bug on the water anywhere near a lurking fish, he'd wheel and take it in a fast, seamless, and impressively vicious move. Usually they'd thrash in one place while I quickly waded over, reeling in line. One or two managed to throw the hook, but I landed most of them.

The biggest one—about a five-pounder—took the bug in thick cover and made a good run with two sharp left turns through the thickest reeds, so that my line was going roughly east, then north, then back west toward open water. It looked like a hopeless tangle for a few seconds, but it was a big fish and I wanted it, so I threw down the rod and went hand over hand down the line to land him. It seemed like a fair catch at the time—it always does with a five-pound bass in your hands—but it did seem odd to release the fish and then go looking for my fly rod. It was a beautiful bass, though: big, fat, solid, and brilliantly green and bronze. Still, it would have been a more traditional job of fish playing if I'd had hold of my rod the whole time.

A ceremonial bass dinner has become a tradition on this trip, so before it was all over, I broke the neck of one good bass and strung him up on a forked stick for supper. (I think if you're going to kill a fish to eat you should do it without regrets or second thoughts, but you should go ahead and *kill* it.) It was a nice seventeen-incher that was comfortably over the fifteen-inch size limit. When I got together with Ed back where we'd left the belly boats, I found that he had also kept a fish. His was just noticeably bigger than mine—maybe an inch longer and fatter—but I'm sure he didn't do that on purpose.

Ed and I talked about this as we hiked back to the truck and drove to the cabin, and we agreed it was fun to know what was going on for once. Largemouth bass now and then get on something like a school of bait fish or a herd of crawdads, but in my experience they are lurkers and brooders and don't often tip their hands. Then again, I'm not what you could call a real bass fisherman. Those of us who think of bass in terms of how they are either like or unlike trout catch them more because they have a temper than because we've figured out what they're doing. That's why we often end up getting them on the most god-awful flies, the best of which look like cat toys with hooks. Some of the spin fishers out there know bass the way a surgeon knows your pancreas. That's another reason to stop and talk to them now and then.

Back at the camp, Ed and I went over to the shed to clean our fish. It was late in the day, when a crowd often gathers, but we were the only ones there and the gut bucket was still empty. It was one of those moments when it's downright glorious to be a fisherman. We did a quick autopsy on the fish to confirm what we already were certain of. Both bass had been caught in shallow water with tadpoles nearby and we knew exactly what we'd find in their stomachs—so we were surprised to see that both fish were full of nothing but dragonfly nymphs.

So much for certainty. But then it's one of the charms of fishing that you can be dead wrong but still be right enough to get the job done. When people say fishing is like life itself, this is the kind of thing they're talking about.

We walked back to the cabin to start supper: Texas-style beer-battered fish, canned corn, and fried potatoes. It was just dark and the wind was blowing so hard we had to hold on to our hats.

Chapter 3

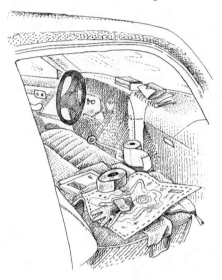

Weeks later, the Nebraska highway map from that bass
trip was still in my pickup, along with the Colorado
and Wyoming maps that live permanently on the dash-
board and sometimes spill onto the floor when I turn a sharp corner. I'd put it away eventually, but that would mean the trip was
really over, so there was no rush.

The maps in the truck pile up over a season, and they add to the
general mess, but it seems to me that maps should be permanent
fixtures in the vehicle, along with the jack, spare tire, tow chain, roll
of duct tape, matches, toilet paper, shovel, ropes, motor oil, jacket,
gloves, knife, notebook, flashlight, fishing regulations, and I don't
know what all else. Like all slobs, I believe that messiness is the natural order of things and that it's not only useless, but also wrong to
fight it.

At this stage of the game, I must have somewhere in the neighborhood of a hundred maps, some stored rolled up in a big wicker
wastebasket, the smaller ones neatly folded and kept in boxes. (I'm
one of the few people I know of who can properly refold a highway map.) There are maps of every state or province I've ever

driven through and more detailed maps of most of the areas where I've fished, hunted, hiked, or camped in the last thirty years. Many are still clean and fresh-looking, but some of the more wrinkled ones have scribbled notes and cryptic Xs next to beaver ponds and bends in rivers. I may not remember exactly what some of those Xs mean now, but I know I've never bothered to mark places where the fishing was lousy.

I like maps because they give me an overall sense of place in a no-nonsense, Germanic sort of way, because they keep me from getting lost some days, and because they tempt me off the beaten track by giving me a pretty good idea of what's away from the trails and behind the fences. It seems like I've spent half my life trying to locate myself on maps, either just out of curiosity or to answer specific questions like "Where the hell am I?" or "How do I get out of here?"

The first time A. K. Best and I went to Labrador, Canada, to fish for brook trout, we each bought copies of the official Labrador highway map. We didn't get these to navigate from—the guides and bush pilots would take care of that—but just to get an idea of where we were going. We were delighted to learn that the province is almost literally trackless. In five hundred thousand square miles of lakes, rivers, forests, and tundra, there is one short rail line and exactly two so-called highways that the tourist bureau charitably describes as "seasonal gravel roads."

One of the beauties of being in genuine wilderness is the knowledge of how far you've come, how far you have to go to get back, and how much empty space there is around you. That's just one of the reasons why you should always have a map.

Not long ago I moved from the outskirts of the small town in Colorado where I'd lived for twenty-two years. The new place is a little farther up into the foothills, three hundred feet higher in elevation, one valley over, and just across the line into the next county. I only had to buy a single 7.5-minute quadrangle topographic map from the U.S. Geological Survey to put together with the county and forest service maps I already had to gave me a pretty good picture of the immediate countryside I'd begun to explore on foot. I was happy to see that my house is on the map: a tiny, isolated brown square on the lip of Rowell Gulch.

When people ask, I tell them I'm seven miles from the old place, but that's by car. When I look at the map I see that it's about three and a half miles on foot, around the back side of Beech Hill, past a rock crag that forms a bird's-eye grain of contour lines on the map, and down Stone Canyon. Or more like two and a half the hard way, down the ridge of Beech Hill, over Steamboat Mountain, and through town. Cars and roads have their uses, but they can royally screw up your sense of where you actually are.

Why I moved from the old place could be a long story, but I'll make it short. The gas station next door sprang a leak in one of its underground storage tanks (thereby violating a whole slew of Environmental Protection Agency regulations) and polluted the surrounding groundwater that fed my well. Susan smelled it first— women almost always have better noses than men—but I smelled it soon enough. Gas fumes were coming out of all the water taps. It was a cold day, but it seemed best not to light a fire in the wood stove.

Susan had moved in there with me several years earlier. We'd met at the daily newspaper in nearby Longmont, where she was an editor with her own desk and I was the fishing writer who shuffled in once a week to deliver his column. You could say it was an office romance, even though I went to great lengths to stay out of the office.

Susan put up with the ratty house without many complaints, but I won't say she "put up" with all the fishing as many men like to say it. The fact is, her family had fished in Michigan for generations, commercially and for sport, so going fishing anywhere, any time, for however long was something she never thought to question. From the beginning, when I said I was going off to fish and couldn't say when I'd be back, she'd say, "Okay, 'bye." This seemed perfectly normal to me at the time and still does, but I'm told it's rare.

Anyway, I went outside, slid the hand-hewn sandstone well cover aside, and dropped a Mason jar into the well on a string. The water sample that came up had a two-inch skim of gasoline floating on top. I took it next door to the gas station and told the manager it had come from my well. He said, "Jesus Christ!" and called someone at what he called the "parent company." I went home and called a lawyer.

Here's where I can make it short, even though in fact it was long and sort of complicated. I sold the house to the company for what it would have been worth before the place was poisoned, plus a little extra for my trouble. My lawyer said it was his duty to tell me this could be worth a million dollars, although it would cost me half of that before it was over and it could take five years, during which all the legal stuff would surely cut into the fishing time.

I told him I had better things to do with the next five years than being up to my ass in a lawsuit, and that as far as I was concerned this was now a real estate deal with me holding an extra card. He gave me a dark look, shook his head, and said I was either extremely sane or a little crazy, he couldn't decide which. He also said he'd never had a client walk away from the money so quickly. I said I'd been walking away from money all my life and it got easier with practice; that in fact most of us don't even *want* money, we just want relief from the struggle for it. That got me another look, followed by a grudging nod.

I should have been heartbroken about losing that house—not that it was anything special. In fact, it was pretty marginal, which is why I was able to buy it outright with a small inheritance left by my father. At the time, it was the cheapest house for sale in the county, and even then I could just barely afford it.

The house was also across the county road from a decent trout stream—that was the real selling point—and since it was pretty rough, it could almost be made to sound like something out of a Currier and Ives print, as in "I live in a little place by a trout stream in Colorado." But it was really just an old frame house next to a gas station, both put up before the days of strict building codes and EPA regulations. Even when I bought it, it was long past its prime.

A friend once described it as "Appalachian," which I decided to take as a compliment.

With no house payments to meet, plus fishing and some hunting, plus a garden and some chickens and cutting my own firewood, I could live for next to nothing (if you didn't count labor), and so I had the time I needed to be a writer. It also kept me from spending most of my time and my best energy trying to bring home wages, an idea that still terrifies me.

For most of our history, we human beings have pieced together a living season by season if not day by day. This whole idea of employment is fairly recent, and I don't think we're quite used to it yet. When you work for someone else, you never feel you're being paid enough for giving up that much of your life and your self-reliance—and of course you're right.

I planted some Russian olive trees and let the yard go wild, partly on principle and partly from laziness. I fixed the things that broke—at least the things I didn't think I could do without—but I never made what you could call improvements. It was a slow, almost imperceptible process, but the old house, which wasn't built any too well in the first place, was slowly but surely returning to the soil.

In the last few years the best thing about the place was the trout stream across the road, but even that wasn't the same anymore. In those twenty-two years, the so-called fly-fishing industry grew and so did the population of Colorado's Front Range, so there were more and more fishermen on the stream as time went by, and the fishing took the predictable hit. Trails appeared where there were none before; the trout got smaller and smarter.

Then the old guy who owned both banks of my favorite stretch closed the stream to fishing. He never explained why any more than he'd explained why he'd left it *open* to fishing for forty-some years. My guess is, it was the number of people fishing it. Once it had just been a handful of locals, but then suddenly there were lots of strangers, some of them well dressed, driving shiny new SUVs, and clearly from out of town. At least I hope that was it, because if it wasn't, then it was a lawyer warning him about the liability exposure of an attractive nuisance or some other legal rat's nest that can make a nice guy think he's being a fool.

There were people who got pretty upset when the NO FISHING signs went up—including some of the strangers—but you could shut them up by asking "What would you do if *you* owned a mile of trout stream?"

Two years after it was closed and everyone got used to the idea that it was permanent, I quietly asked the guy if he'd lease that stretch to me and some friends. Actually, I did it through an intermediary. I'd fished there and lived within walking distance for over twenty years, but in the grand scheme of things I was still seen as a newcomer by the old guard, and this was the kind of thing that would sound better coming from a native. The answer was "I'd rather not," and that was that.

I loved that old house by the creek and lived a mostly good life there, but things were changing. There was more traffic (at least by small-town standards), a stretch of my home water was posted, and the house itself was beginning to come apart at the seams like a worn-out piece of luggage. I'd actually said out loud a few times (just to see how it sounded) that maybe it was time to unload it and move someplace a little wilder, quieter, and farther from town. I meant eventually, sooner or later, but as usual the gods took it literally, fouled my well, and said, "Okay then, here you go."

Soon after we moved out, they cut down all the trees I'd planted—some of which had grown from seedlings to forty or fifty feet—tore down the house, and hauled away the wood and the wreckage. I waited to feel bad but only thought that if they hadn't knocked the house down, it would have fallen down of its own accord soon enough. Then I briefly worried that I'd gone cold inside (it can happen). But judging from the political and personal squabbles I was into at the time, my emotions still seemed to be as active, unpredictable, and as close to the surface as they'd ever been.

That was four years ago. I'm still waiting for something like anger or sadness to hit, but I'm beginning to suspect it never will. I should have felt mowed down by progress—and I suppose I was—but then why should I be any different from anyone else? It was all too clearly meant to happen, especially since I came out of it living in a better place. I realized that it was the country and the streams around here that are home, not so much the house.

Of course, I can't help but wonder how that stretch of creek is doing now that it's gone for eight years without seeing any fishermen. Eight years is a good long lifespan for a brown trout. By now, a whole generation of them would have grown up there pretty much unaware of the existence of humans, let alone artificial flies. But "I'd rather not" was clearly intended to be final. I imagine the stream being like it was when I first fished it more than two decades ago: an overlooked corner of the world with fat trout and not another soul in sight. I'd give anything to know, but permission is not forthcoming and I refuse to poach it, even though I know the place so well I could get in and out undetected without half trying.

So Susan and I moved to the new place, up the North Fork and then on up a dead-end valley (where the road goes in but doesn't come out the other side), and into the next drainage. It's not right on a trout stream—by now a place on the water is way out of my price range—but it's a ten-minute stroll from one creek and a two-minute drive from another, which will have to do. It's another old house, but in better shape, and it sits on a bigger piece of land that's occupied most days by some cottontails and a small herd of mule deer. Every place has a signature bird, and here it's the pinion jay. Now and then, usually in winter, a flock of between twenty and forty of them descends on my feeders and empties them in minutes. The house itself is heated by three wood stoves, backed up by solar, backed up by propane: a model of self-sufficiency.

When I filled the propane tank the first fall, the co-op guy said, philosophically, "Propane: buy it or freeze." I pointed to the solar panels aimed at the south-by-southeast sky where the sun shines in the winter; I pointed to the three neatly stacked cords of firewood. He shrugged, as if to say, One little subsistence hippie isn't going to change the way things are.

The co-op guy is a new acquaintance; so are Ron the bulk water guy, Kelly the wood guy, Leon the horse guy, and a few others, but we're still part of the loose community that calls the little burg of Lyons its town and that's neatly broken down into a sort of local tribal structure. Officially, we're now part of those Blue Mountain People, who are known to be aloof and standoffish, but not to be confused with those Spring Gulch People, who are even more reclusive.

Still, I eat breakfast at the same cafe, hang out at the same fly shop, and am still marginally involved in local politics, even though I can't vote in town or even in that county. On the other hand, I have developed a kind of emotional distance, so I can now say, in my standoffish, Blue Mountain way, "It sure is a shame what you people down here have to put up with." And of course there are still the half dozen old goobers who, every time they see me in town, have to ask, "How come ya ain't fishin'?"

Maybe it was the move shaking things up or maybe it was just a coincidence of timing, but not long after we settled in the new place, Susan also started her monthly newspaper: the one people in town had been urging her to do—against her better judgment, she sometimes says. Everyone we knew agreed that the local rag had gone stale and that a new paper was needed, and since Susan had been a working journalist for years and a section editor at a nearby daily paper, she was seen as the only one qualified to do it. It's called the *Redstone Review* because our historic local industry is the quarrying of red sandstone.

I liked the idea because it seemed like a romantically doomed, idealistic venture (the people who saw newspapers as going concerns sold them off ten years ago), but then I could like it from a distance because I didn't have to do the work. I'm just an occasional volunteer copy editor, paperboy, and spiritual advisor, and I write a monthly column that could be loosely described as social commentary. Actually, the first few were called "Humor," but then several in a row weren't very funny at all, so instead of firing me,

Susan just changed the headline to "Insight." One of the advantages of living with the editor.

Doomed or not, the paper has been a hit. It's pretty to look at and it's eclectic, with contributors including a writer of mystery novels, a former *New York Times* reporter, a fishing writer who's gotten a little out of his depth, and correspondents from as far away as New Zealand. We've even made the local establishment press, the news hook being: Imagine, in this day and age, a town of less then two thousand people with three stoplights, a square-dance band called Poultry in Motion, and two newspapers. (I should point out that Lyons has always provided comic relief for the rest of the county.)

So, as quiet and peaceful as it is out here, Susan's office does amount to the newsroom of a small publication, and so there's a kind of hustle that develops around press time. I don't take part in it much, but I do notice it between fishing trips. Susan's phone rings constantly, she's at her desk for hours at a stretch—usually with a cat on her lap and another draped on the warm computer with its tail dangling inconveniently over the screen. And she often wears a hot pink T-shirt that says, NOT TONIGHT, HONEY, I HAVE A DEADLINE. Other than that, life hasn't changed all that much.

And as it turns out, there's a stretch of a small feeder creek not too far from here that can be reached on foot through an angular patchwork of public national forest land. It was the second thing I noticed on the new map, after locating the house: the thin blue line snaking down the foothills, far from any road and well hidden by private land. I didn't just discover it at that moment, in fact I've always known it was there in a general way. I'd crossed it on county road bridges miles above and miles below the stretch I'm talking about, so I knew where it came from and where it went, but, uncharacteristically, I'd never wondered what it did in between. That's probably because in years of fishing in this part of Colorado, I'd never talked to anyone who'd fished it or who was even willing to say if there were trout in it.

I also knew it was a moody little thing. In rare years it will go virtually dry, with bleached rocks and pitiful trickles running between the pools, but then here and there along its length there are swimming hole–sized tubs where trout can hold over, and up in the dark, forested canyon the water would stay cool enough even in midsummer.

And then in other, just as rare years, it blows out. A decade ago it flooded in a wet spring and ate a sturdy bridge a few hundred yards from where I now live, stranding several families higher up the valley. For the better part of a week the poor kids couldn't even get to school.

It's a fact of life, as streams tend to be, but local fishermen don't pay it any mind and visiting fishermen don't even know it's there. Some old-timers have told vague stories of trout being caught up there back in the mythological old days, but, as I said, I'd never talked to anyone who'd actually fished it. As I traced the little creek's course on the map, I was suddenly embarrassed that I'd never fished the thing myself or even just walked its length to see what it looked like. It was so close, so unknown. What the hell had I been thinking all these years?

So my friends Rick Breeze and Don Lutter and I decided to hike up there and check it out. It was early in my first spring in the valley, and I thought the creek might be too high and muddy with runoff. But it wasn't too bad down at the bridge. The water was just a little off-color, but not so much that I couldn't spot an eight-inch brown trout in the bridge pool, and between there and where we were going were some feeder creeks that would add volume and silt, so above that it might not be too bad.

I didn't agonize too much, because this wasn't a real fishing trip. It was more like a scouting expedition that amounted to an excuse for the best kind of hike: the kind with a purpose but not enough of one to matter. I brought a fly rod anyway, on the premise that only a fool would walk miles to a trout stream without one.

It was a fine hike. The weather was breezy, drizzling and a little on the cool side, although wearing even a light rain slicker got me overheated and sweaty from walking, and I could see right off that

I was going to end up wet one way or another. Still, it felt good so soon after winter.

The country between here and the creek is that dramatic, ponderosa/juniper foothills landscape, punctuated by house-sized boulders and lush, mossy little seasonal watercourses trampled with elk tracks. It was all rainy grays, browns, and olives with the odd brilliant splash of color from yellow prickly pear flowers, purple ball cactus, and blue moss campion. This was the season of pre-runoff—or maybe early runoff—when these semiarid foothills are as green as they ever get. In most normal years, it turns dry in late spring and even as the streams swell up and turn brown from snow melt out of the mountains, the surrounding countryside down here begins to turn brown from thirst.

I looked at birds (juncos, chickadees, Steller's jays, a red-breasted nuthatch, a hairy woodpecker, a raven, a Townsend's solitaire). Don, a strong walker, set a serious pace. Rick, a geologist by trade, looked at rocks and hit the ones he liked best with a little hammer.

We had two compasses and two maps: one from the U.S. Geological Survey showing nothing but topography, the other from the Bureau of Land Management filling in federal, state, and private boundaries. The hills get pretty craggy in there, and there were game trails but no human path, which is a hopeful sign, even though it makes picking a route more difficult. From the top of the first ridge it became obvious that the short way was really the long way—an uphill and down backbreaker. Better in the long run to follow the contours and add a mile.

We also had to negotiate around some private in-holdings. Without going into my usual tirade, I'll just say that I'm every bit as sensitive about trespassing as I am adamant about my right to go on public land. This is a view I've come to later in life, but, like all converts, I now take it seriously.

It took a little longer than we thought. We got to the creek late in the afternoon, with not much time left before we'd have to start back. Seems Rick had promised to cook dinner for someone and didn't want to be late. He didn't explain further, but it sounded important.

It was a pretty little stream: down in the ponderosa pine and Douglas fir between steep hills; the kind of place that might get an hour of direct sunlight on the longest day of summer. At that point, the creek was about twelve feet wide at a more or less flat spot and obviously a little out of its banks. By the time the runoff came down and it cleared enough to fish a dry fly, it would probably lose a few feet in width. As it was, the water was running a little high and off-color, with maybe ten or twelve inches of visibility.

We'd come into it at a flat run with a brush jam on the downstream end: small willow and dogwood limbs, but not the logs or tree trunks that a bigger stream could move. Above that the canyon turned sharply and there was a good, flat bend pool against a moss- and lichen-covered rock cliff. (Maybe granite or basalt. I should have asked Rick.) Upstream from that was loud pocket water running unfishably white and foamy out of a narrow canyon. That was as far as we could see without wading across and hiking on up. We decided not to do that because none of us had waders and we didn't want to hike out wet to the crotch.

By the map, we were right at the confluence with Burnett Gulch. The gulch was shown as intermittent—a dotted blue line— but right then it had a good head of nearly clear water in it. This was exactly the spot we'd been aiming for, so I penciled the route on the map while memory was still fresh.

The big forested bump to the north northwest would have to be Round Mountain. Downstream, roughly east, was a half square mile of private land, although it wasn't fenced on this end. (I like getting far enough into the country that people don't feel they have to outline everything with barbed wire.) Upstream was a good two miles of stream on national forest; steep, twisty, thickly wooded, and hard to reach. The access from above that was blocked by more private land. There was another route in from the north, but that would be longer by a few miles and steeper, so you'd have to come in on horseback to save time or do an overnight camp.

So this was it: a hard-won, little-known stretch of public water that might or might not have fish in it. Far out.

It would have been enough just to have found the way in to it, but then I'd carried a three-piece fly rod several strenuous miles in a drizzling rain, so I said to Rick and Don, "Give me a few minutes, okay?"

Rick looked at his watch and said, "Sure, take your time."

I rigged up a size 8 dark stone fly nymph with some lead weight on the leader and a yarn strike indicator. I didn't have more than a few minutes, and that was the closest I could come to the brutal efficiency of a gob of worms and a bobber. The stream was a watery, coffee-with-cream color with dirty foam lines along the edges of the currents. I told myself it was fishy-looking.

Of course, there's a psychological component to this. That is, you fish better with faith than without it, although in a pinch curiosity will work, too. I fished as well as I could given the circumstances— just a little better than going through the motions—and after about ten minutes of casting to foam lines and current edges I hooked and landed a little rainbow.

It was only about nine inches long, but it was bright and fat and still had parr marks down its sides. It was a healthy, well-fed young fish that probably had larger relatives living in the same water, although how *much* larger would be anyone's guess. One trout after only ten minutes in a single pool with cold, muddy water. Not bad. This could turn out to be a "sleeping beauty," the name cartographers give to blank spots on maps.

Don is one of my rare nonfishing friends. When I landed the trout, he trotted over and looked at it as I held it in the cold water. He said, "Jeez, that's pretty. It's a little one, isn't it?"

CHAPTER 4

It was mid-May and I was driving down a back road in Pennsylvania trout country with two bamboo fly rod makers: Walt Carpenter and Mike Clark. We were between streams and several days into the trip, so the usual urgency had dropped to a tolerable level and the conversation had begun to drift into topics slightly more general than when and where the next hatch might be.

In fact, at that moment the conversation had drifted into what was currently wrong with the sport of fly-fishing. Never mind the particulars, which I don't remember now anyway. This is just something older fishermen sometimes do, especially those who either make or fish with split bamboo rods and therefore think of themselves as, in Carpenter's words, "the caretakers of a tradition."

Periodic bitching is an unavoidable symptom of a lifetime spent fishing: Older fishermen have been around so much beauty for so long that perfection seems ordinary and even a single beer can tossed on the bank of a stream looks like pure ruination—and this from men who, in our younger, wilder days, carelessly disposed of some empty beer cans ourselves. Of course, now we pick them up, possibly as a kind of penance.

We had just slowed down to go through one of those little two-block-long rural towns that consist of a gas station, a dozen small houses, and a couple of genuine white picket fences. Whoever was talking (was it me?) was in mid-rant about something that was wrong with fishing when two young kids came whipping out of an alley on bikes. Their blue jeans were wet to the knees, they were laughing hysterically, and they were carrying fishing rods.

The talk stopped and we watched them go by; all three of us trying to see if they had any fish. Then someone said, "Yeah, well, never mind," and it was back to what hatches we might find—if any—on the next stream. It was the right time of year for Sulphurs and maybe also some March Browns, but things had been slow, so there was no telling.

That spring it had rained for six weeks straight, swelling up the streams; then it cleared and turned humid and hot, with daytime temperatures in the nineties. By the time Mike and I arrived, the streams were high and muddy, the hatches were off, and the whole state felt like a steam bath. People said it was the worst spring for fishing in the last twenty years.

And yes, we knew that before we came, but the trip was planned, Mike and I were hot to go, and there was the possibility that things would turn around while we were there. I mean, conditions improve in fishing about as often as they go wrong. The one thing you can always bet on is that things will change.

Mike and Walt spent our first full day there out in Walt's shop, a small, terminally cluttered barn behind the house. Clearly these two, who had never met face to face before, wanted to sit down and talk things over. They're both bamboo rod makers and they're both sort of opinionated, but otherwise they're about as different as you can get.

Mike is a self-taught craftsman from Colorado—a successful upstart Westerner—while Walt, who may not mind being called an old-timer in the bamboo fly rod business, fairly reeks of Eastern tradition. He worked for two of the great old names in bamboo—Leonard and Payne—and then built his own rods using the old F. E. Thomas milling machine, a deafening Victorian monstrosity that dates back to the turn of the last century and seems to work as well as anything newer.

They talked about bamboo suppliers, aging, and heat treating, moisture content, node placement, whether or not to pin your ferrules, and the ins and outs of the bamboo rod business, which is so underground and word of mouth that, if you didn't know better, you'd assume the possession of a bamboo fly rod was a felony in most states.

Normally I'd have chewed through my leash if the first day of a fishing trip had been spent sitting around talking, but the outlook for fishing seemed so poor I almost didn't mind. We did finally get out for a few hours after supper that day. Walt's friend Carl Roszkoski showed up and we went over to Fishing Creek, where we all got skunked.

Over the next few days we went from Fishing Creek to Big Fishing Creek to Spruce Creek to the Little Juniata River to Spring Creek. They were all running high and fishing poorly. We saw some pretty country and met and fished with some good local fishermen, all of whom apologized for the condition of the streams as if they had anything to do with it.

For the most part, we had good company and the fishing stank—which happens—but we did all have our moments. One evening on the Little Juniata I pulled out of a blank day by catching five small fish on a dry fly in the last desperate forty-five minutes before full dark. Four of them were brown trout, and one was a sucker. I counted the sucker privately and reported "five fish,"then started to feel bad and fessed up to the one bottom feeder. Someone kindly said, "Well, he was feeding on the top when you caught him, right?"

And one day on Spruce Creek, Mike noodled a fat twenty-inch brown out from under a bridge on a huge, cone-headed Woolly Bugger. There were four of us that day, all stubbornly fishing dry flies, but no one really held it against him, probably because he was using a bamboo rod.

• • •

That was our first trip to Pennsylvania. We were invited back the next year largely because we hadn't whined about the poor fishing, which is, after all, much more common on even the best waters than any of us care to admit. Sometimes bad fishing in a good place sours you and you go looking for something else. Other times it just makes you want to go back.

So we were back in Pennsylvania about two weeks after Rick, Don, and I had hiked into that little stream near my house that, only a few warm days later, had gone into full, brown runoff. One of the best things about traveling to fish is the way you can hedge the seasons, stretching them out in one place and condensing them in another. At the same time that the freestone streams in the Rocky Mountains are blown out with runoff and all but unfishable except with bait, the streams in Pennsylvania are at their best—or at least they're supposed to be.

As it turned out, that second trip was everything the first wasn't: We had sweet, mild spring days, clear streams (or as clear as those limestoners ever get), regular mayfly hatches and spinner falls, and enough bank feeders eating ants and inchworms to keep you out through the middle of the day.

A. K. Best came along this time, and when we all started catching fish right off the bat, Mike and I told him that we'd paid his dues along with our own on the last trip when we'd fished on so bravely and stoically in the face of bad conditions. That was crap, of course. Poetic justice is as rare in fishing as it is anywhere else. It was just persistence: the same thing that lets even a blind pig find an acorn now and then.

The same Spruce Creek that had been a brown mess the year before was bright and quiet; running clear with that limestone chalky color in the deeper pools, and there were lots of trout eating Sulphur mayflies in the single-minded, but unhurried way of well-fed fish.

We were fishing at the Spruce Creek Club, where Vince Marinaro used to belong, and it was a little more highbrow than what we're used to, with its palatial old clubhouse, landscaped grounds, and the long line of matching bentwood rockers on the front porch.

The club dates back as far as Walt's milling machine, to the days when a captain of industry might say to a farmer, "This is a nice little trout stream you have here. How much do you want for it?"

There was a mob of seven of us by then: Walt, Carl, A.K., Mike, and me, plus Bob Budd and Charlie Meck. Bob is the one who kindly got us in as guests at the club, and Charlie, of course, is the bug guru and author of *Pennsylvania Trout Streams and Their Hatches*. It's a book that's not unknown even in the West, but I saw tattered copies of it on the front seats of every fishing car I looked into in Pennsylvania. That's deeply impressive to a writer.

We'd fish casually during the day, and then after a good sit-down supper at the clubhouse, we'd go back to the creek to wait for the Sulphur spinner fall. It was all so civilized that Mike, A.K., and I would now and then look at each other and roll our eyes by way of saying, "Will you get a load of this?"

Down at the creek, Charlie would sit on a bench and read *The New York Times* until we started to see swarms of spinners forming in the air. Then, when the rest of us picked up our fly rods, he'd grab a butterfly net and catch bugs. "Aren't you gonna fish?" I'd ask, and he'd say, "I fish here all the time."

This part of Spruce Creek flows through open deciduous woods, and it's been so thoughtfully manicured you don't notice it at first. But then you keep coming to pools where, although there are trees everywhere, there just don't happen to be any right where your back cast has to go. Most of the cutting was done so long ago that even the stumps have rotted away, so unless you really stop and think about it, this just seems like a happy coincidence. I guess this is how the other half lives.

I saw my first March Brown hatch a day or two later on Penn's Creek. They were beautiful mayflies: tan marked with brown, elaborately speckled wings, sort of like miniature Brown Drakes. A.K. and I caught a few and had a long discussion about how we'd design a new fly to match these bugs, even though there are already a hundred years' worth of patterns on the books for this hatch. The difference between us is that A.K. would remember what he'd said and tie the flies when he got home.

I had some store-bought March Browns in my vest, but as it turned out, the fish were letting those flies go by and sipping the same old Sulphurs. Charlie said the hatch had just started, so the fish weren't used to the new bugs yet and would probably ignore them for a while. It sounded plausible.

Like most of our days in Pennsylvania, this one was all about hatches and dry flies. For much of the time, little or nothing happened, and we were all hesitant to fish nymphs. Then the bugs came off and it was all business. Trout were rising, we all caught some, and the long walk back to the car was mostly in the dark. By then I had gotten over my delight that the same quill-bodied Sulphur duns and spinners we fish in Colorado also worked in Pennsylvania. Well, maybe I hadn't actually gotten over it, but I had at least stopped giggling every time I tied one on.

We slept at the Spruce Creek Club again that night, four to a room, and once again the snoring got so bad Mike had to take his blanket and find a quiet couch downstairs. When we checked into a motel somewhere near Big Fishing Creek the next night, Mike slapped his credit card on the front desk and said he wanted a single room as far from the rest of us as possible. By then the rest of us had dwindled to Walt, Carl, A.K., and me—almost a reasonable number. The woman behind the counter glanced at us. We'd been fishing for days and looked it. She turned back to Mike and said, "Of course, sir."

By then we'd fallen into a steady routine. We were fishing late for the spinner falls and then sometimes driving for what seemed like hours looking for someplace to eat supper. Maybe rural Pennsylvanians are so tough they can eat anything, or maybe we just had rotten luck, but the food was almost always bad. The low point came at a truck stop where I had the worst chicken-fried steak of my life. Try to imagine a slab of Spam dipped in pancake batter and deep fried in donut grease.

By the time we hit Spring Creek, we were tired and seasoned, and we'd caught a lot of trout. I couldn't tell you how many or how big they were, but there were as many as you'd expect from a week's worth of good fishing, and some were as big as you'd hope for from famous streams. Interestingly enough, no one complained about what was wrong with fishing, because nothing *seemed* wrong. If one of us found a beer can, he'd squash it, put it in his vest, and keep fishing.

By then I think Mike, A.K., and I had come to feel a little like Pennsylvania fishermen. That kind of thing happens on any trip where you don't fall in the river, don't make any hideous social blunders, and manage to catch some fish. We weren't, of course. We would never have the lifetime of accumulated detail behind us that makes for home water, but in the limited, momentary way you come to understand a place on a trip, it began to seem more familiar than not.

During the days on Spring Creek we'd stalk around looking for those quiet, occasional risers tucked up under the banks in the shade, so we could try for them with something like an ant, a beetle, or an inchworm. This is sort of a lazy business anyway, and these fish are hard to spot, so you go so slowly that if someone saw you they might think you were doing nothing at all; just standing around in the woods holding a fly rod for some reason. That's what it feels like when it's a long time between fish, and it's not all bad in a lush, green forest with a cool breeze, echoing bird songs and the promise of a good evening rise. There's no use being frantic when there's nothing to be frantic about.

And in the course of quietly watching, we'd all had our little revelations. At the beginning of the trip we'd all done what you do in a strange place: We'd stopped at the nearest fly shop to buy the local flies we didn't already have. In this case, inchworms, gypsy moth larvae, and March Browns. We may not have known what to do with them, but it's a required ritual.

Then one day Mike was watching a big rainbow rising quietly along a bank. The fish was sipping something off the surface, probably small ants that were stuck in the film and all but invisible to humans. He was agonizing over what fly pattern to tie on when a single blade of green grass drifted down the current. The trout rose confidently, ate it, and then spit it out. Mike tied on a bright green floating inchworm just as confidently and caught the trout on his first cast. Twenty-one inches and fat as a muskrat. He said it was the first time in his life that he'd ever fished that fly.

The deal on Spring Creek is that it's strictly catch and release, not so much to preserve the fishery—although that's the effect—but because the water is so polluted with chemicals like Mynex and Kepone that eating a fish could either give you cancer or cause brain damage, I forget which.

That can be an intensely weird thought if you dwell on it too much, but I noticed that I didn't. The fish are big and happy—apparently unaffected—and they're hard enough to catch that it can take all your wits to get one. You spend a lot of time in the fisherman's trance, which is a comfortable enough place to be. Fishing is one of the few ways I know of to let go of the past, forget about the future, and live in the moment. And living in the moment is the only way I know of to accurately understand life without getting pissed off.

So we'd wander around during the days looking for bank feeders and then, in late afternoon when the Sulphurs started to come on, we'd begin to see trout doing those quick rolls a little way out from the far bank. These weren't the soft, offhanded rises to ants or beetles, but the first hungry takes to mayfly emergers that meant the hatch was beginning. Often those first fish would be in the shade of some overhanging vegetation. Maybe it was a stand of mountain laurel instead of the ponderosa pines and junipers I'm used to, and maybe some of the unfamiliar birdsongs were just pretty gibberish, but those were just interesting details. Everything else seemed entirely recognizable.

The first night on Spring Creek, A.K. caught three or four nice fat brown trout from a good pool and then hooked a real big one that ran him downstream. By the time he'd splashed through a shallow riffle, gone around a bend into the next pool, and landed the fish, he'd been gone for ten minutes. There'd been a guy upstream from him watching all this, and when A.K. walked back up to the pool, he fully expected to find the guy fishing it. But he wasn't.

So A.K. waded over to the man to say thanks for saving him the pool and to ask how he was doing. "Not too good," the guy said. Turns out he was using a #22 mayfly dun, figuring the fish were eating something small because he couldn't see anything on the water, not realizing that the bugs were bigger, but they were lying flat on the surface so you couldn't spot them.

A.K. took out one of his #14 Sulphur spinners and handed it to the guy. "Try this down in that pool," he said. Then he walked back to the car to see if the last cup of coffee in the bottom of the thermos was still warm. It was the kind of thing he'd do. Two of the lessons I've learned from A.K. are: Be generous when you can and quit on a good fish.

I heard the story from A.K. that night and then ran into the same fisherman on the stream the next evening, although I didn't know it was him at first. "Doin' any good?" I asked. He held up the Sulphur spinner. It was chewed up pretty badly by then, but I still recognized it as one of A.K.'s trim, handsome flies. He said, "I been doin' great ever since some crazy old guy gave me this yesterday."

Some crazy old guy. I was gonna have fun with that.

CHAPTER 5

Have you ever started reminiscing with a friend about a fishing trip and found that you remember things differently? I have. Now and then it's downright puzzling, but usually it just amounts to slightly different versions of the same story, as when one witness says the mugger was five eleven and another says he was six one, but they both pick the same guy out of the lineup. Mike and A.K. have both mentioned things about that last trip to Pennsylvania that I don't remember. That's not to say they didn't happen, just that they didn't register with me, or maybe they happened while I was in the bushes taking a leak. Some of the things I recall have also drawn blank looks from them, although with me being a writer and all, the assumption is that I'm imagining things.

It's a common prejudice and one that's probably not entirely unfounded. After all, someone once defined fiction as just something a writer made up and nonfiction as just something a writer made up using the names of real people. More to the point, novelist John Irving once said that a memoir is, by definition, what the author remembers, not necessarily what happened.

You can go to your fishing journal to prove things like the year, the month, the weather, the hatches, the name of the guide, and maybe the weight of a big fish if someone bothered to bring along a scale. But if you're like me, the things that stick aren't written down. And memory is flawed. Fishermen know that better than anyone, we just don't always know how much.

We do know how it happens, though: You land a nice fat six-teen-inch cutthroat that the guide you're with swears is twenty inches long. You know what he's doing and you know why he's doing it, but unless there's a tape measure handy, you don't know it beyond a shadow of a doubt—and he is a professional, after all—so you say, modestly, honestly, "It ain't over eighteen."

Or let's say you're fishing a mountain creek that's known for small brook trout, but you've hiked way up in there where, you've heard, there are some deep holes and the fish are bigger. They are, and there are lots of them; they're easy to catch, and it's a beautiful, cool, rainy day with the spruce forest so lush and green you feel like you're fishing through an enormous salad. Maybe you see a golden crowned kinglet perched on a twig no more than a foot away, and then later you glance upstream and spot a huge mule deer buck in velvet. You're doing well enough that you quickly lose track of how many fish you catch, and although you admire the biggest, handsomest ones, you don't measure them. The walk out is long but downhill and pretty much effortless.

Back home they say, "How'd you do?" and you say, "Good," which is true enough so far. But then they say, "Yeah, but how many and how big?" You give an accurate estimate, carefully paring away all the beauty and good feeling and getting right down to nothing but bare facts, right?

The same thing can happen when you tell someone about an argument you had last week. There's some emotion loose in the story—a different kind than you get from fishing, but emotion nonetheless—and you've had a while to stew about it. When you quote yourself as saying not so much what you really said, but what you *should* have said, you may be vaguely aware of it at the time, but the moment it's out of your mouth it becomes the truth. The thing is, fishing stories, war stories, and love stories are all the same: There's more there than just the facts, and when the facts get in the way, they can become expendable.

It works in reverse, too. Most years I fish a lot; maybe not as much as some, but more than most. At the end of a good season I'll have fishing licenses from four or five states and a couple of Canadian provinces, some worn-out fly lines, near-empty fly boxes, a born-again thriftiness, and a good tan. But then on one of those cold, solitary late-November walks, I'll get to thinking about that one beaver pond I never made it to and think, What the hell did I do all year, sit on my ass?

And of course fishermen hear what they want to hear. Maybe you say, "Well, I got a five-pounder, but just the one. Most of them were more like a pound and a half or smaller, but it was real pretty, and there was no one around, and the guide was a real comedian. And that five-pounder was something. Here's a picture of him."

The guy looks at the snapshot and envisions a river crammed with five-pounders—so many you could cross from bank to bank on their backs and not get your feet wet. You can see it in his eyes. If he ends up going there himself, he'll come back and say, "It wasn't as good as you said it was."

I've given this some thought, and I think my standard recollection of fishing is made up of the emotion of the moment, the mood of the day, the scenery, the company, the weather, who I am, who I think I am, who I'd like to be, my own sense of poetry, and a few tattered shreds of what actually happened. As James P. Carse once said, "What we see depends partly on what is there and partly on who is looking."

Maybe I'm the only one who does it that way, but I don't think so.

I once fished with a man on a good local river. We weren't exactly in each other's hip pockets, but we were within sight all afternoon, close enough to shout encouragement or trot over to look at an especially pretty fish. And the trout there really *are* pretty. They're bright rainbows with wide red stripes and a strain of cutthroat in their lineage that gives them iridescent gill covers and orange slashes on their jaws.

The way I remember it, I caught six or eight trout, the biggest maybe fifteen inches. He got about a dozen and his biggest was an honest seventeen, measured from little finger to little finger on two outstretched palms, which on me is just a hair under eighteen inches. And we did it all on size 18 Blue-winged Olive duns and emergers, which somehow makes it better.

But then at a cafe on the way home, a guy at the next table spotted us for fishermen and asked how we'd done. My partner said he'd caught no less than thirty trout, including several that were at least twenty inches, if not longer. He believed it. He looked at me with big chipmunk cheeks and the most innocent smile I've ever seen and said, "Right?"

I said, "Yeah, right. The guy kicked ass," thinking: Okay, I know he did better than me, but did I underestimate my own performance that much? Not likely. Fishermen don't do that.

I don't think he was knowingly lying, either. We weren't close friends, but he hadn't struck me as one of those chronic bullshitters (he actually seemed a little on the shy side), and he'd have no reason to think I'd back him up in a god-awful lie to a stranger.

Out in the parking lot I waited for him to say, "Man, we really pulled that guy's leg, didn't we?" but he never said it. What he said was, "That was one of the best days of fishing I ever had."

We all think we're good observers, or at least that we can believe our own eyes, but few of us have ever been tested. I had a philosophy professor back in college who staged a great demonstration on the relationship of facts to experience. In the middle of a normal class one day, several people stormed into the room, got into a loud argument with the professor—complete with swearing and shoving—over who was supposed to have the room scheduled for that hour. Then they stormed back out and slammed the door loudly behind them. It had been sudden, surprising, and borderline violent, sort of like catching a big fish.

The professor turned to us and said, "Okay, write down your best account of what just happened."

Naturally, it had all been scripted and rehearsed with some people from the drama department, so he knew every gesture and word. There were twenty of us in class and the elapsed time between the actual events and our retelling of them worked out to a matter of minutes. None of us got it right, and better than half of us got it terribly wrong.

That was the year I finally realized that the nature of knowledge was such that you couldn't know anything for sure, but then if *that* were true, you also couldn't know for sure that you couldn't know anything. I finished up the semester and got my degree, but my career in philosophy was already over.

So maybe we can't even be sure that what happened five minutes ago is what actually happened, and the more time that passes the more you have to wonder. I think that's just a simple storage problem. People now like to think of their memories as computers with only so many bytes available, so that eventually you have to dump some old files to make room for all the new stuff coming along.

I'm more comfortable picturing my mind as a rolltop desk with only so many drawers and cubbyholes, but the same principle applies. Consciously or not, you hold on to what seems best and treat the rest as junk mail. Eventually a trip where a few big fish were caught becomes a trip where nothing *but* big fish were caught. And how big were they? Well, the guide said even the little ones were twenty inches.

Of course, all those countless days when no fish were caught begin to dwindle to a single distilled example, so that, if pressed, you'd have to say you do remember getting skunked once, but you can't quite remember where or when. You don't do it on purpose, but eventually your life as you recall it becomes a work of fiction based loosely on actual events.

I've become more aware of all this as I've gotten older and the desk has gotten more cluttered, but I think I knew it in my twenties, too, because when an old fisherman once said to me, "Boy, I've forgotten more about fishing than you'll ever know," I didn't doubt it for a second.

Not long ago A.K. and I were sitting around on a back porch in Alberta, Canada, with some other fishermen telling some well-worn, thirty-year-old stories about our friend Koke Winter. Koke is legendary in some fly-fishing circles. He was A.K.'s mentor years ago back in Michigan, and he was never shy about it, either. Once someone asked Koke if he knew this talented fly tier named A. K. Best. Koke said, "Know him? Hell, I *made* A. K. Best." When A.K. heard about that later he said, "Yeah, that's about the size of it."

Anyway, these are stories that involve monumental feats of skill and sportsmanship and trout of incredible size. One of those huge trout was mounted and then later scattered all over West Yellowstone, Montana, some years back when the fly shop it was hanging in blew up from a gas leak—making for a poignant end to one of the stories and, incidentally, destroying the evidence.

I've been told that A.K. and I sometimes tell a pretty good story together, playing off each other, swearing to each other's facts, supplying each other's punch lines. Maybe we do, especially after a good, long day of fishing when the one of us who still drinks has had a few stiff ones and the other is enjoying what we used to call a contact high.

We have told these stories dozens of times on dozens of back porches, and we both believe them to be absolutely true. More than that I cannot say.

CHAPTER 6

By early July, I'd taken to making almost daily visits to a big fish spot I know about. It's on the upstream side of a narrow bridge over a trout stream near here where a couple of boulders jut out into a riffle from the left bank. In normal summer and fall stream flows, the rocks divert the current off to the side and then swing it around into a small but deep backwater tight to the bank. The bleached snag of a dead tree hangs out over the pool, and on shore, also hanging well out over the water, there's an impenetrable multitrunked narrow-leaf cottonwood intertwined with a smaller bigtooth maple bush.

It couldn't be a better spot for a trout. There's shade, cover, deep water, a tongue of slow upstream current, a long, shallow riffle above that pumps dissolved oxygen and insects into the water, and it's a tangled mess, with every approach blocked in one way or another. The only way you can even see into it is by leaning over the bridge railing twelve feet above it and a little downstream, although you have to lean at the right angle so you don't throw your shadow on the water and scare the fish.

Of course, it's unfishable from any angle in any stream flow:

something I've determined after years of observation in all seasons. I guess that's why I've never bothered to get permission to fish there, even though I probably could if I made the effort. If you lived the ideal life, you'd be reborn as a brown trout living in a place like this.

I don't know how many times I looked into that pool from the bridge before I saw the trout I figured had to be there. It was an early summer day and there were some small, dark caddis flies on the water, so instead of just glancing admiringly at the pool as I walked across the bridge, I stood there for an extra few minutes until a big brown rose gently and took a bug. By "big" I mean about sixteen inches in a stream where a foot-long trout is considered a pretty good one.

I was alone and I don't actually remember it, but I assume I laughed out loud when I saw it because people tell me I do that. (I guess after a childhood spent lowering worms out of sight, it still astonishes me that you can actually *see* a fish.) Then I waited another minute or so for him to eat another bug, just to make sure I really had seen it.

I know now that by the time this happened the runoff had come down enough that the rest of the canyon upstream was fishable. It took me a while to put it together, but the bridge pool finally became the spot I use to gauge that on this fork of the creek: When it looks right, it means that the flow in the twenty-some miles of creek in the canyon upstream has dropped enough for the trout to start eating dry flies. I already had places like that for the north and middle forks and the main branch of the same stream, but none of them was quite as sweet and tantalizing as this one.

The bridge above this pool is on one of my regular walking routes, right at the mile-and-a-half mark, making it a three-mile round-trip. I try to do a two- or three-mile hike every day I'm not fishing or doing something else strenuous. I do it for health, discipline, peace of mind, and just to be around a trout stream for an hour or so without fishing it.

I think that's good for me. When I'm not trying to catch fish from a stream, I can look at it without the usual greed and calculation. That is, I can look past it a little and appreciate it in a larger way, which seems worth doing.

In this stretch the creek pours out of a steep, pine-forested canyon and begins to spread out through some flatter pasture country. A sparsely traveled two-lane runs along it, and I usually park at the bottom and walk up the road, past Richie's place, where a mountain lion ate a couple of his goats last winter, past the mown acre where Vince Zounek gives casting lessons, and up along a high red sandstone cliff.

In the early mornings of hot summer days, this is where you go into cool shade, and with the air refrigerated by the stream and the breeze that always blows down the canyon, it can feel more like September than July. You'll often hear the seven or eight clear, descending whistles of a canyon wren in there: one of the prettiest and most distinctive birdsongs I know. Even on a bright morning it sounds contemplative, and on one of those cool, dark days when a drafty canyon feels like a room in a ruined castle, it seems to change to a minor key and get downright sad.

A few other people walk this road, and we always nod and say hello, but most days I have it to myself, which is how I like it best. I've also made a few animal friends: some assorted dogs, plus a horse named Bobby Socks and a mule named Poncho who likes his forelock scratched. It may not be entirely healthy, but most days I'm happiest talking to something that won't talk back.

This place is also a study in the birds that are found along Western trout streams. The country here goes quickly from open ponderosa pine forests to mountain mahogany and cliff-rose shrub lands to lush trout stream riparian habitat with cottonwood, box elder, American plum, water birch, bigtooth maple, and such. Poison ivy and wild-grape vines climb the cliffs in spots, and there's the odd feral apple tree left over from the orchards that grew around here a hundred years ago.

Don't worry, I won't list them all, but in a season of walks you can see half a guidebook's worth of birds in a mile and a half, and sometimes in the fall, when the apples begin to drop off the trees, black bears come and gorge on them, get bad cases of what my dad used to call the green apple two-step and leave amazing piles of bear shit on the road.

A few years ago, a woman who lives along here called the county sheriff. She said there was a dead deer at the end of her driveway and that a black bear and a mountain lion were fighting over it. The sheriff said, "What the hell am *I* supposed to do about it?"

I'd been walking up there a lot, maybe three mornings a week, because it was early July and the stream should have been out of runoff.

It wasn't, though, because it had been a rainy year, so I'd been passing the time trying to learn the songs of warblers. I've always been a visual birder, but getting a good look at a four-inch-long bird up in the broadleaf foliage of a cottonwood is like trying to spot a kitten in a room full of open umbrellas. Or maybe like trying to see the subtle rise of a trout in fast pocket water under dappled shade. I was using the straightforward method for learning birdsongs that an old bird-watcher friend recommends, namely, "When you hear a bird singing, go see what it is."

This is the same kind of thing you do in fly-fishing. You pay attention, piece things together, learn to actually see what you've been looking at all along, and sooner or later you no longer have to be beaten over the head before you understand what's going on. This can take a long time; longer for some than for others. I've been at it for better than half a lifetime and there are still days when I think I miss more than I see, although how much you've missed is yet another one of those things that you can never know for sure unless there's someone to point it out.

You know: You thought you saw something, but you're not sure, so you assume it was just your imagination, while the gnarly, seasoned fishing guide standing next to you says, "That was a sixteen-inch rainbow trout eating a size 18 Pale Morning Dun emerger an eighth of an inch below the surface. And by the way, that twittering you hear is a yellow warbler."

But I don't watch birds as practice for trout spotting, even though it may turn out to be just that. I've been training myself not to see anything as practice for anything else, but as some kind of an end in itself, on the premise that if you do what comes naturally for its own sake, it'll all fit together by itself eventually.

It had been a good fishing season so far. In April, before the runoff started and when it was still snowing now and then in the high country, I fished the local streams and did okay, sometimes even on small dry flies. We don't get much in the way of early hatches on these local freestone creeks, but flies do peter off, and when the water is low and clear and the trout are hungry, they'll sometimes come up for a #20 Wulff or Hare's Ear Parachute.

While the runoff was roaring at home, Ed and I did the bass and pike trip to Nebraska and then A.K., Mike Clark, and I fished the limestoners in Pennsylvania. In late June I was in Alberta with A.K., where the streams in the Red Deer River drainage were in perfect shape and the Pale Morning duns and Green and Brown Drakes were on. We met some helpful local fishermen, told some old stories out on the back porch, and one evening A.K. and I agreed that every American should visit rural western Canada once a year just to be reminded how to act.

A damned good start to the season; better than most, actually, and more expensive, too, but that's just how it worked out. Good fishing and money both just seem to come and go, so you might as well enjoy them while they're here.

Lately I'd been fishing the local bass ponds and some trout lakes either side of the Colorado-Wyoming border, doing well some days and getting impatient about the stream in the canyon, while telling myself that if fishermen have one virtue, it's that they're patient.

One day I was driving down to the fly shop in town to catch up on fishing reports and local gossip when I saw a kayaker on foot. I had actually gone past her and around a bend before it registered—a dripping wet woman walking down the road carrying a life vest and a paddle—so I turned around and asked her if she needed any help.

She wasn't hurt or even shaken, but she'd lost her boat and needed a ride down to the take-out.

She said, "I'll get your seat wet."

I said, "It's been wet before."

She said, "It wasn't really that rough, there was just no relief," which sounded like a fair description of any number of things.

Anyway, it was another sign: When the stream is high enough for kayaking, it's still too high to fish.

I cracked a sweat walking up to the bridge pool the next morning. It was already in the eighties and by that afternoon it would hit ninety-six on my back porch thermometer. When I came out of the shade of the cliff just below the bridge, the morning sun was backlighting the white, feathery seed plumes on the mountain mahogany bushes, and for a split second it looked like hoarfrost on a bitter January morning.

I met a panting chocolate Lab out walking his human, and it occurred to me that a strange Labrador retriever gives you a better greeting than almost any person you know. I mean, how many of your friends run up to you wiggling all over and lick your knees?

The mountain mahogany was beautiful, the dog was fun, and although I don't like hot weather much, I know it blows out the snowpack in the mountains and makes the streams drop, so I was happy enough.

The creek was clear but still high. The current was rolling over the rocks and boiling up white in the bridge pool. When it's right, the lip of the biggest rock is dry, the current cuts a loop to the left and the pool is a smooth lopsided disk; rotating slowly clockwise, sometimes with a big trout just visible through the leaves and the bleached, dead limbs of the snag.

Not that it's always been the same trout. As I said, I guessed the first one I saw there at around sixteen inches, and in the next few seasons he grew to something like eighteen and got nice and wide across the back. Then he was replaced by an ambitious thirteen-incher that had grown to about seventeen inches by last summer.

I wondered if he was still there.

I wondered if I'd break down and fish the spot if this one cracked twenty inches. A brown trout that big from this stream would go down in local history, although I'd have to have the dead fish in hand to be believed.

I haven't tried so far because it seems impossible and because I enjoy leaving the fish alone for reasons I haven't really bothered to examine. And also because once I can see him I know that whole, beautiful canyon upstream is down and clear and the trout are ravenous for size 12 Dave's Hoppers.

For some reason there's just not much pressure when it comes to this particular trout. On the other hand, I haven't entirely ruled out trying to catch him.

I'm not sure about the ethics of this, but I think I could just manage it if I went in now and took a few limbs off that snag with a handsaw. Not all of them, just enough to allow for a Hail Mary sort of half-dapping pile cast with a little downstream hook.

Okay, maybe I could make the cast and maybe I couldn't, but I can *picture* it. I could consult Vince, my casting guru, for some pointers, and maybe even practice on the lawn with an old hula hoop for a target. The sweet spot would be no bigger than that. It would be a single cast and if I buggered it up, I'd spook the fish. The drift would be tricky, too, and even if I pulled all that off, I'm not sure how I'd play him out into more open water where I could handle him. Of course, I could come back the next day, and the next. Once I started I could never stop. It could conceivably ruin my life.

I'd probably tie on the local variation of the Elk Hair Caddis, or a size 14 Royal Wulff, or maybe the good old Dave's Hopper. The fly pattern would hardly matter. Fish have died of old age here without ever seeing an artificial fly.

CHAPTER 7

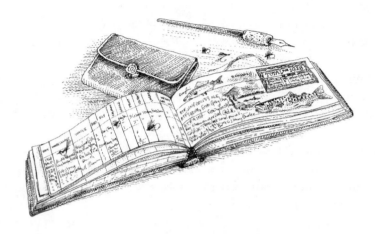

I haven't made any entries in my fishing journal about that trout under the bridge because of a conversation I once had with Bob Scammell, a writer friend in Alberta. We were trying to decide what constituted a fishing trip (this seemed important at the time). I said I thought the definition could be pretty loose, maybe even poetic, but that you probably had to go to water with a fly rod and at least have the intention of making a few casts. So, as interesting as it might be, standing on a bridge without a rod and watching a trout probably doesn't count.

I started keeping a fishing journal again six years ago after a hiatus of almost a decade. The old journal, which was none too formal anyway, seems to have petered out right in the middle of a fishing season, and I don't remember why I stopped writing in it. Maybe I forgot, maybe I got tired of it; more likely I just got lazy.

For that matter, I'm not sure why I started it up again either, except that keeping a journal or log is an old tradition with both anglers and writers. Many individual fishermen and guides like to scribble down a few rough notes for future reference after a day on the water, and they can come in handy. I know of one guide who pared down his working fly selection to a single, small box after keeping notes on what patterns worked for a few seasons.

Fishing lodges and clubs have been known to keep meticulous records of fish caught going all the way back to day one. The idea is that a detailed lodge journal kept for long enough can tell you if the fishing in a particular area has declined, improved, or stayed the same over the years, what the best weeks are on average, when the hatches come and go, the most productive fly patterns, the best weather and flow to fish in, which spots are best when and all kinds of other things, including—eventually—a sense of history.

An individual fisherman's journal does the same thing, but usually not as well because it wanders around to different lakes and streams at different times of year. But if you fish a lot around home or make annual trips to favorite spots, you can eventually accumulate some pretty useful stuff.

A writer's journal can be useful, too, but it has more potential pitfalls. I mean, maybe you really did have some great thoughts that you never did anything with and have since forgotten, but you're just as likely to go back through an old journal and learn how simpleminded you used to be or that you actually haven't had a fresh idea since 1969.

Of course, for a journal to be useful to a fisherman it has to be accurate, and we're all just as likely to brag in print as we are in person. I know of at least one camp in Canada that keeps two separate logs: one that it lets the fishermen write in, and another—kept by the head guide—that actually tells the truth.

One afternoon when we were stuck in the cabin by weather, I got to thumbing through the log. It was full of enthusiasm, humor, failed attempts at humor, long detailed descriptions of scenery, fish and the northern lights, a sketch of a fly and even an overwrought poem. There was plenty of evidence of people having fun, but not much information.

But when I asked to see the guides' log, the head guide obviously didn't want to show it to me. He shoved his hands in his pockets, looked at the ground, and began to stammer out an improvised excuse. I guessed that this journal also contained comments on the sports, possibly including me, so I let it drop. He seemed relieved.

Fishing journals are pretty personal items, and what you write in yours is your own business. A technician will fill in all the nuts and bolts information in excruciating detail, looking for that single juxtaposition of air and water temperature, light, season, hatch, and moon phase that will make every fish in the river a pushover. It really is worth looking at because these things can happen, although there are usually more variables than even the most disciplined diarist can keep track of.

A scorekeeper will painstakingly add up the total number of fish caught, maybe even their lengths and weights, and enter it at the end of the year. Then he'll ponder it. He might compare it to years past or divide it by the number of days or hours fished or even figure out what he'd have made that year if he'd sold all his trout for five dollars a pound. Probably whatever number he comes up with will seem too small.

A closet poet might forget to mention if he caught any fish or not and fill the page with observations about the beauty of nature and the meaning of life. This stuff will seem brilliant at the time, but later it will read like greeting-card copy. Believe me.

I've talked to fishermen who only keep journals of trips to exotic places as souvenirs, and others who only record what happens on their home waters where they stand a better chance of building up a useful body of information.

Some of us pore over our past journals looking for average hatch dates, best flies, or some other secret. Others hardly ever look back but get some satisfaction from just putting a year of fishing down on paper.

You have to wonder what eventually happens to these things. In a perfect world, a detailed journal on a certain river would be passed down to someone twenty or thirty years younger who fished the same water and still cared what the fishing was like way back when. That surely happens sometimes, but I think it's more likely that old fishing logs end up in a box of stuff in the garage where they're forgotten for years and then finally disposed of.

Not long ago a friend gave me an old fishing log that she bought at a garage sale for fifty cents. The title page says, "Happenings around Clark's cabin on the Laramie River." The first entry is dated September 5, 1960: "First weekend in new cabin. Worked like hell cleaning and scrubbing it. Full moon. Water low & clear. Caught limit between 10 am and 3 pm on Sunday—several better than 12 inches." A good beginning.

The journal ends abruptly 122 pages and thirty-eight years later with an unremarkable entry dated June 11, 12 & 13, 1998. "Up by myself. Put in the new shelves. . . . River already falling and clearing. Fishing should start next weekend."

And that's it. In the universe of Clark's cabin on the Laramie River, next weekend never came.

The journal is written in a blank, ruled law record that's bound nicely in blue leather—the kind of book that's meant to last—and it was taken care of. It's not dusty, there are no pages torn out, no coffee stains or cigarette burns. It was sold a scant three years after the last entry for less than a dollar to a woman whose only interest in it was that she had a friend who fishes. So how did it come to that? Loss of interest? (That seems doubtful.) Catastrophe? Death? Maybe there were no kids to pass it on to. Or maybe there were, but fishing bored them to tears.

I suppose if I read the thing carefully, cover to cover, I could form a theory of what happened, but it doesn't really matter. The real lesson is that you should write whatever the hell you want in your journal because chances are no one's gonna care.

When I dug out that old journal I stopped keeping, I found it to be a little heavy on the philosophy and a little light on what I wanted to know, which at the time was: When did the bluegills start biting at Sawhill Ponds ten years ago? I wanted to know that because it seems like they come on later now than they used to but, unbelievably, that old journal was only dated by the year. It told me how I *felt* about the bluegills biting (I felt good, apparently), but not when it happened. Now I'll just have to trust my memory, even though that's getting risky.

All the stuff I wrote about life, death, sport, and beauty was mildly interesting and some of it still rang true, but it did seem to go on and on, and, honestly, I didn't really give a shit how a younger version of who I am now once thought about anything. I just wanted the facts.

So in the new journal I'm allowing myself to speculate about the nature of existence as much as I want (for some of us, that's unavoidable), but only after first noting the date, place, time, weather, flies used, and fish caught, though not necessarily how *many* fish.

It hasn't been easy, but so far I've stayed honest. I can now look back to last year and see that on the cloudy afternoon of May 7, with a light breeze and temperatures in the high seventies, the bluegills were biting a size 10 chartreuse damsel nymph from one till about four-thirty. And, yes, the green young cattails and budding cottonwoods were real pretty and yadda yadda yadda.

Like anything else, a fishing journal can also have unforeseen uses. For instance, at the end of last season, during the first good snowfall, I started feeling like I hadn't gotten in enough fishing that year. I won't go into why. But then I went back through my journal and found exactly 201 pages worth of fishing for the season and felt a little less sorry for myself.

And it wasn't lost on me that the worries, complications, and tragedies that had kept me off the water were not recorded. At the most they were only hinted at by some mysterious gaps in the fishing. Even now, with some of it still fairly fresh, I can't match every blank spot with its appropriate trouble.

In a book review in *The New York Times,* Josephine Humphreys once wrote, "What an author doesn't say, and why he doesn't say it, are the heart of the book." I doubt that's true of most books, but it describes fishing journals perfectly. There's day after day on the water with an unseen life somewhere in the background. The only clue as to what it's like is the frequency of the fishing trips, and that's not much to go on.

Actually, there's a longer list of things that *shouldn't* be in a fishing log than of things that should. Stay away from business. Stay away from politics, except maybe as they apply to fisheries management. Stay away from your friends' troubles, except maybe to note cryptically that old you-know-who was in sort of a pissy mood because of you-know-what. After all, journals have been known to fall into the wrong hands.

And keep away from your own troubles, too. (If you don't, you'll go back through the thing years from now and be embarrassed at all the whining.) I know that in the time covered by one of my logs, two of my fishing friends took their own lives. That could have legitimately been part of the journal, but it's not and that's just as well. Some things should be left without anniversaries to observe, and I sure as hell don't have to be reminded how I felt at the time.

(On the other hand, I should probably make a note somewhere reminding myself that I hadn't offered either one of those guys advice for at least six months prior to their deaths.)

Usually a good fishing log just amounts to some useful information, maybe with a little homegrown therapy thrown in, but now and then one can rise to the level of art. Between October 23 and 29, 1994, writer Dave Hughes kept a journal of a solitary trip to Big Indian Creek in eastern Oregon. It turned out to be a rambling account of fishing, camping, traveling, and other things that often reads like poetry (with good fishing tips included). In 1996 Stackpole Books published it as a little hardcover book called, naturally, *Big Indian Creek: October 23–29, 1994.*

If you enjoy quirky little monographs, it's a real gem, but if you're worried about the literary quality of your own journal, it could be discouraging.

Actually, I think it's a waste of time to think of your journal as art. Art is public, but a journal is private, which is why the classic diary has a lock on it. The only person who ever has to read it is your most forgiving critic. You will see published journals now and then, but I've always suspected that those were intended for publication all along or that they were extensively rewritten.

But if you want to *see* a fishing journal that became a work of art, try to find a copy of *Muriel Foster's Fishing Diary,* published in 1980 by the Viking Press in a leather-bound, full-color facsimile edition, and later in a paperlock edition from Penguin Studios.

According to the introduction, Muriel Constance Foster was a classic Victorian sportswoman. She was born in England in 1884, attended the Slade School of Art, lived in the English countryside, and for most of her adult life, fished with a fly rod.

This fat diary covers the years 1913 to 1947, and it's hard to describe. Typically, the left-hand pages have the usual dry notes on dates, species, and numbers of fish caught, fly patterns, and such, while the facing pages, under "remarks," have notes and sketches done in pencil, pen, and ink and, as often as not, meticulous watercolors.

That's the basic format, but then the sketches usually scatter themselves across both pages in an apparently random way, and sometimes they cover both pages like a mural. It seems as though any time there was enough blank space, Foster filled it with drawings and watercolors. Some are beautiful finished compositions that could be framed if they were bigger. Others are quick sketches that are just as perfect in another way.

There are landscapes, portraits of wildlife, dogs, fish, insects, cottages, fishermen in boats, farmers, ghillies, odd pieces of tackle, a house cat, a weather vane, a leather bag hung from a branch, you name it. She also had the habit of not only listing the fly patterns that worked—mostly fancy trout and Atlantic salmon flies—but of also making perfect thumbnail watercolor illustrations of them.

And I mean perfect. The flies are painted to scale, so that a Butcher is less than a half inch long, while a full-dress Silver Doctor is more like an inch and a half, and as far as I can tell, they are flawlessly accurate even through a magnifying glass.

This is not a book you read; it's one you graze through when you're in sort of a vague good mood. You flip it open randomly and read that between June 25 and August 3, Foster and Roddie McKenzie fished the Dundonnell River, where they caught trout on Zulus and Blue Zulus—both illustrated in color in the column marked FLY. In the columns for SEA TROUT and VARIOUS, a water ouzel perches on a rock in the river. On the facing page you read that McKenzie "hooked a salmon or enormous trout, which nearly pulled him in." (Since we don't know if it was a trout or a salmon, we have to assume he didn't land it.) Above that is a colored pencil drawing of a black and white dog sleeping next to four dead brown trout with the river in the background. It looks like early evening, with a dark sky and purple hills.

In a strange way, this book is one of the most revealing looks at an angler's life I've ever seen. It works like real memory—part verbal, part visual, only partly linear—and the cold information, like numbers and size of fish caught, takes a backseat to what you could only call the experience. This is what we'd all secretly like our journals to be: beautiful enough to be worth preserving, even if no one knows or cares who we are.

It's also a kind of heartbreaker because, while most fishing journals stop abruptly or slowly peter off into blank pages, this one actually ends. Toward the back of the *Diary*, when Foster was in her sixties and her arthritis was becoming debilitating, the handwriting looks more labored, and the sketches, though still good, are fewer and less detailed. The number of fishing trips also begins to decline and the entries are shorter.

There are no drawings on the last page, but Foster describes what you have to think of as the last place she fished. It was, "A very deep, black little lake, surrounded by trees or cliff." She said it was difficult to fish, but that it was, "a most beautiful lake." Below that she wrote:

"Finis
Arthritis!"

CHAPTER 8

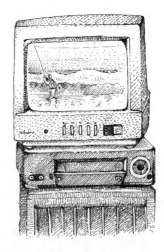

I was in one of the fly shops down in Boulder picking up some fly floatant and some fresh tippet material. As I said, it was shaping up to be a good year. I'd already burned through a bottle of Gehrke's Gink and two spools each of 4 and 5x tippet, and the season wasn't half over yet.

It was just a quick stop, but for some reason it struck me how much fly shops have changed in the last few decades. For one thing, there are a lot more of them now (in some big fishing towns they're on almost every corner, like gas stations), and I seem to recall a time when you couldn't buy clothing in a fly shop. Now some of them are more like T-shirt boutiques that sell some expensive tackle on the side. I've been told this is the only way to "make your nut" these days. The shops also open much later in the day. Once upon a time, fishing stores catered to people who were out at dawn.

They've also become weirdly similar, like chain restaurants. You'll often find the same flies by the same overseas industrial tiers and the same graphite rods by a handful of manufacturers. Even the slogans on the T-shirts are the same: THE WAY TO A MAN'S HEART IS THROUGH HIS FLY, KISS MY BASS, and so on.

My sister once told me a story about a husband and wife who drove across the country with their three-year-old son. They figured the kid would get bored, but he loved McDonald's, so every night they stopped to eat at one because they thought that would give him something to look forward to. It went well enough until the third night when the kid said, "Dad, how come we drive all day and still end up at the same place?"

Don't get me wrong: I love fly shops, I'm glad they're there, and I go into them often to happily spend money on things I really need, but I sometimes feel the same way when I go into a new one. How come I drove all this way and ended up at the same place?

But the biggest change in fly shops is in how beginning fly fishers are treated, which is better now than it used to be.

When I took up the sport, you simply went down to the local hardware or sporting goods store and bought the cheapest rod, reel, and line they had. You only got a few flies, because they were expensive—as much as fifty cents each—and you stayed away from the small ones because they didn't seem like much for the money and they looked like they'd only catch little fish anyway.

Fly patterns were a toss-up. There weren't as many then, but there were still too many to choose from, and the guy behind the counter knew more about duck hunting than he did about fly-fishing. I remember buying Royal Coachmen and McGintys because they were real pretty. They worked, too, but it turned out that other patterns sometimes worked better.

Then you'd go out and flail around on your own until you began to get the hang of it.

There were a few instructional books around and they weren't bad, but they never seemed to start right at the beginning, and when *you* were right at the beginning, they could be incomprehensible.

Fly-casting classes were almost unheard of, and home videos hadn't been invented yet. If you were lucky, you'd find a more experienced fisherman to show you around a little, or at least a succession of kindly older guys out on the stream who'd now and then wander over and set you straight about a few things.

After a season or two of fishing, you'd go back and read the book again, and this time it would make a little more sense.

There may not have been an actual fly shop nearby, but if there was you'd eventually find it and it would be tantalizing and mysterious, like the first real bar you ever walked into. There were odd gizmos displayed in glass cases, strange animal parts hanging on the walls, and a distinctive odor you finally identified as mothballs. Everyone but you seemed to know what they were doing.

Some of the people there would be helpful in a vague sort of way, but there was always the air of a private club about the place, and no one knew quite what to do with a rank beginner except smile wisely, remembering themselves back in the day. You'd feel like the inevitable tenderfoot in a John Wayne movie, with most of the frontier philosophy going right over your head.

One way or another, you learned how to fly-fish anyway.

Since then things have swung about as far as they can go in the other direction with beginning, intermediate, and advanced classes in casting, fishing, fly tying, rod building, and sometimes even entomology, plus specialized seminars, demonstrations, retreats, and shelves full of instructional books and videos.

(I came late to fly-fishing videos and I still haven't watched a lot of them. The ones I *have* watched were just fine, although video fishing seems a little like movie sex: fun to watch, but a long way from the real thing.)

It's probably all for the best—there's nothing wrong with getting a leg up on it—but I still think it takes a long time to learn how to fly-fish well. I once saw an ad for a morning "crash course" in fly-fishing prior to a half-day guided trip in the afternoon. It's probably not a bad idea—any guide will tell you it's better than going out with someone who doesn't know which end of the rod to hold—but it also risks reducing a sport that can take years to master to "Hey, let's take a day and learn how to fly-fish."

The fact is, casting lessons are great as long as you understand that you can learn how a fly rod works on a lawn, but you only learn how to *cast* out on the water with an actual fly tied to your leader instead of a piece of yarn. Books and videos can be great, too, but they're static and can amount to what Neil Postman calls "information without proper instruction." Pure information just lies there on the page or scrolls robotically across the screen, where you either get it or not. Proper instruction comes from an instructor: someone who can change tactics when he looks into your eyes and sees that the light hasn't come on yet.

I was in a fly shop once when a guy walked up to me and asked how long it took to get really good at this. (He may have thought I worked there, or I may just have looked like an old fisherman who'd know something like that.) I said, "Ten years, if you fish three or four times a week." His face fell. He was thinking a couple of weeks, tops. The face of the clerk who was signing him up for a few courses fell a little, too. I tried to save it. I said, "Well, that's how long it took me, but I didn't have much help."

That was true, I really *didn't* have much help, but learning how to fly-fish on your own wasn't all bad, either. You spent a lot of time on the water; maybe not catching fish, but nonetheless out on the water where it all happens, seeing the hatches and spinner falls you'd only read about, spooking trout, and thinking, What the hell were they doing there? and just generally wandering around and getting a feel for the places fish live. With any luck you were young and footloose, unaware that your time was worth anything more than what you happened to be doing with it at the moment.

There were things you reasoned out for yourself, some that came from books and snatches of free advice, and others you learned through a process of elimination: by doing it every possible wrong way first. And there were the things you picked up quickly: wading safety, poison ivy identification, the peculiar habits of rattlesnakes.

A lot of it sank in slowly, but it did sink in, and in most cases it stuck. You also began to feel at home on the water, maybe even more at home than when you were at home. This would hit you the hardest when you were alone. You'd begin to see how simple life could be if you never had to explain yourself.

Most of the people I now fish with have been at it for longer than they can clearly remember, and although they'd have saved themselves some of those early struggles if they could have, they're kind of nostalgic about them now. It's fun to look back on being an idiot now that you think you're smart, and telling about your early train wrecks can amount to a backhanded way of bragging: as if you're so far past that now, it's like it all happened to someone else.

There was also something unforgettable about being young and dumb, in the middle of the worst day of fishing you'd had so far and, at that precise moment, running into the kindly stranger who says, "Excuse me, son. Do you mind if I make a suggestion?" Years later it occurs to you that you are now supposed to be that helpful stranger, not because you've become so wise, but because you've finally learned how to offer advice without being condescending.

Fly-fishing could seem overwhelming then because you couldn't find much help. It can seem overwhelming now because there's so much help available you don't know where to start. I once heard a beginning fly fisher say, "Jeez, I just want to catch a couple of fish and the people at the fly shop are trying to teach me brain surgery." Thirty years ago he'd have said, "I need to learn brain surgery and everyone just says, 'Don't worry. You'll pick it up as you go along.'"

You can say the same about tackle. There's some wonderful stuff out there now, but it's not *all* wonderful and there's probably way too much of it. For instance, at last count there were over seventy makes of fly reel available in the United States. I remember when all I wanted to do about a reel was move up from an American-made Pflueger to a British Hardy (and then maybe to a Bogdan if I could ever afford it), although I can't say why. To this day, I don't think I've ever lost a fish that I could honestly blame on the reel.

Rods may be a little out of hand, too, although the truth about them hasn't changed: That is, some are definitely better than others (and you can't always tell by what they cost), but if you know how to cast, it's hard to find one that actually doesn't work.

There are so many specialized rods out now that you can come to think you need a different rod for every different fishing situation. (That's not your fault; it's how they're marketed.) I happen to agree with Tom McGuane, who said that you can do all the fly-fishing in North America with two rods: a 6-weight and an 8-weight. He also said that a rod had better have a very good reason for being shorter than eight feet or longer than nine.

But tackle is compelling stuff, and most of us who now have ideas about simplicity arrived at them by the long route. It's interesting how many of my older friends have said to me in the last few years, "You know, I've owned dozens of fly rods, but that old eight-foot fiberglass I started with is as good as any of them and better than some." On the other hand, none of them seems to be even a little bit sorry about going through all those other rods (and reels and lines and waders and flies and whatever). The fact is, if you develop the kind of jones I have for fly-fishing—and it can happen—you'll probably spend enough on gear in the next thirty years to have sent a kid to college. And you won't regret any of it, either, although you might miss your ex-wives from time to time.

Eventually you may begin to pare things down a little by carrying fewer flies, settling on a couple of all-around rods with old-timey medium actions, and maybe even passing on the newest high-tech waders for now because so far the patches are still holding on the old ones. You'll probably do this later rather than sooner because it won't occur to you that you don't need everything until you've already owned everything at least once.

You may begin to assume that everything old is good and everything new is worse, and where you used to worry that you were being left behind, you now begin to hope to God that you *are* being left behind. Then one day you'll go fishing with some younger guys and it will occur to you that your tackle is a little dated. Not obsolete—I mean, it still works and all—but it's definitely not next generation. Chances are you won't run right out and upgrade, if only to avoid another trip to the greed mill, but you will grudgingly pick up on some of the newer stuff once you've seen it work—and once you've carefully determined that it's the gear that makes the difference and not the skill of the fisherman.

A friend of mine said recently, "I don't know what some of these young fly fishers are doing, but they can sure catch the hell out of trout." Actually, they're doing pretty much what we're doing, albeit with unfamiliar flies and funny-looking tackle. It's just that some of them are doing it better.

Most days I'm a perfectly happy fisherman—it's my mission in life—but now and then I do catch myself making old-guy noises about how it is now as opposed to how it once was. I used to worry about that because I dreaded turning into a geezer, but then I thought, What the hell, you might as well embrace what comes next because what else can you do?

Once I told a young fly-fishing guitar player I know that I thought fly-fishing was getting to be like rock and roll: more about glitz than substance. I was proud of the succinctness of the phrase. When most fly fishers complain, they go on and on.

He told me I was wrong about both music and fishing: That in fact plenty of rockers were playing for free or for drinks and tips, or kicking it out in basements and garages; pissing off the neighbors for the sheer joy of it—just like they've always done.

And the same goes for fly fishers. Young and old, quietly fishing on unfashionable waters and doing it very well with a handful of flies and perfectly good, but cheap tackle from Cabela's and Kmart. You don't notice them, he said, because they don't show up on the covers of magazines and they don't write books about it.

Then he suggested we go look at this little mountain lake I'd been telling him about, the one I thought was just as good now as it had been back in the old days.

This is why you should always have some young friends.

CHAPTER 9

I have a soft spot for cutthroat trout—any kind, any place. Taken together, the various races of cutthroat are the native trout of the Mountain West and—nothing against the Midwest, where I was born and raised—this is the first and only place where I've felt comfortably at home. Some of us are born where we belong and grow up as true natives; others have to break loose and go find their spot. Apparently, this is mine.

Cutthroats are known for being hardy in some ways but delicate in others. They can live well in sparse, cold waters without much food and weather long, brutal winters, but they're also too easy to catch for their own good. They need clean, pure water—which is harder and harder to come by—and they don't compete well with introduced species of fish.

So, what with too much fishing pressure, dewatering and pollution and the introduction of rainbows, browns, and brook trout, cutthroats tend to hold on in high, quiet, remote, rugged places that are beautiful to see and hard to reach. There's a good deal of romance to that, and underneath the macho and the technique and the lust for size and numbers, most fishermen are still romantics.

That summer I got a pretty good dose of cutthroat trout fishing on a trip to British Columbia. We were fishing for west slope cutts—a few as big as nineteen and twenty inches—that were still living in the drainage where they'd evolved. They had that hand-in-glove perfection of true indigenous fish. They were fatter and prettier than seemed possible, and their camouflage was so suited to the aquatic landscape that sometimes you couldn't clearly see a big one even as you were reaching for him with a landing net. The fishing pressure in the area had steadily increased over the last dozen years, and the trout were no longer so easy that you could almost feel guilty about catching them, but they hadn't quite lost their typical cutthroat innocence, either.

It was a fine trip, but in the end all it accomplished was to put me so deeply into cutthroat head that after I got home I didn't really want to catch anything else. So the first thing I did—after decompressing for a few days—was hike up to a little cutthroat lake in a Colorado wilderness area with the guy who'd teased me about my crotchety attitudes about music and fly-fishing. In fact, now that I think about it, that whole conversation may have been his way of wangling an invitation. If it was, he got me good.

I've known about this spot for something like thirty years—long enough that it seems like I've always known—and I try to get up there at least once every season as an observance. I think of it as a secret spot, and I'm proprietary about it in a paranoid, suspicious sort of way. I've shown it to a handful of people over the years, but only after I determined they were okay (as if that were up to me). And even if it's not as secret as I'd like it to be, it *is* one of the few places I know of that hasn't changed enough that you'd notice in almost three decades.

I took the guy there because I trusted him to appreciate it, treat it well, and keep it under his hat, which is all you can ask. And anyway, I thought he had it coming. He was young—just out of his twenties—and he had a profession, but he'd recently quit his job because the fishing was good and he wasn't getting out enough. As it turned out, he fished away the summer, hunted away the fall, and by December he was still living the sporting life with no visible means of support. His only comment in all that time was, "Shitty jobs are a dime a dozen."

One of the things that's always protected this little lake is the trip in. It's a long drive on a road that was always bad, but that's gotten worse in the last ten years. Then it's a longer uphill slog through steep, rough country: It's the kind of place where you can put in a twelve-hour day for three or four hours of fishing. It's also the kind of hike that hurts. At my age, it's easy to imagine myself running up there like a gazelle when I was in my twenties, but the fact is it hurt then, too. I remember that clearly. I may stop to rest an extra time or two now, but that's not the kind of thing you should dwell on.

It's a nice touch that there's perfectly good fishing lower down, some of it conveniently within sight of the four-wheel-drive road. There are also some larger, better-known lakes nearby with decent trails right to them. It also helps that the lake has no name, although on the best topographic maps of the area there *is* a small blue dot right there where anyone could see it.

Something else that's guarded this place is that, although it's just pretty as hell, it doesn't look like much of a trout lake. Actually, it's *not* a lake, at least not technically. It's just an oversized wide spot in an alpine meadow where two small creeks come together, made wider and deeper by an ancient, impacted logjam at the outlet. The jam has been there for decades and seems solid to the point of permanence, but it's still a temporary structure that could—and eventually will— blow out in a bad spring runoff. I think about that, and every time I come around the last bend in the trail I hold my breath. I assume the lake will still be there, but I understand there's no guarantee.

This lake or pond or whatever you want to call it looks pitifully shallow and sterile when you first see it. Actually, it's deeper than it looks—you learn that when you wade into it—but it's still proba- bly not over twelve or fourteen feet at its deepest. The bottom is rust-colored rubble rock and fine silt that has a faint blue-green glacial cast in the sunlight. The water itself is so clear it creates an optical illusion: The color of the bottom doesn't change at all with depth, so it looks like a uniformly foot-deep puddle that couldn't possibly support trout.

Everything up there is like that. The lake lies in an open bowl of mountains, and when you look west toward the twelve-thousand-foot bare rock peaks at the head of the valley, your eyes insist that they're only a thousand yards away. The map, however, says they're two miles off and two thousand feet higher. It's disorienting at first. When you're new to this country, you can decide to stroll over there and have a look around that next ridge and end up on a five-hour death march. But with practice, you come to grasp the true scale of things.

It even happens with sound. On a clear, windless day, you can hear the brittle clattering of rocks breaking loose from those crags and rolling down the distant scree slopes. This is the sound of the Rocky Mountains slowly but surely falling apart, and it can sound so close you'll look around, startled, expecting a rock to land at your feet. I'm not the first one to notice this. Annie Dillard once wrote, "The mountains are great stone bells."

In a way, the whole place is an illusion, possibly including the idea that it doesn't get fished much. The trail in is unmarked, faint, and easy to lose in one or two places, but there *is* a trail. I'm sure some people come just for the view (it's worth the walk), but the fact is, trails to mountain lakes are pounded by fishermen.

If you spend the time to look, you'll find some old fire pits, although none of them has seen much use recently. Off to the side of one, there's the inevitable pile of tin cans so old and rusted they crumble to dust when you try to pick them up and pack them out. There was a time, long before the area was designated as road-less wilderness, when a rough logging operation went on in the valley and there was a road of sorts that you can still see traces of. It was never possible to drive right to the lake, but you could get a vehicle close enough to hump in a week's worth of canned food.

But aside from that old pile of cans, I've picked up only two pieces of trash in three decades: a brittle snarl of monofilament heavy enough to land a tarpon and an empty salmon egg bottle.

I've also found a few flies hanging in the trees, but as poorly as some of them were tied, I couldn't think of them as garbage.

As for the fishing, not only hasn't it changed since I started going there, but it actually seems to have gotten a little better. That's just an impression, but it's probably a correct one, since a fisherman's natural tendency is to think things were better back when and worse now.

I hold on to this little lake as proof that although things often end up going to hell, they don't actually *have* to. But I still hold my breath because I know anything could happen. Not much of a bump in fishing pressure could badly hurt the fishery. (I still wince at the two fish I killed for dinner there years ago). A season of god-awful snow could shut out the sunlight and winter-kill the lake. Deep snow melting quickly could blow out the logjam and leave a narrow trickle surrounded by five acres of sand. Acid rain could slowly strangle the whole aquatic ecosystem, and a spike of acid snow melting all at once in the spring could do the same job quickly. This is all stuff that not only could happen, but probably will sooner or later, so that the longer the lake seems permanent, the more fragile it becomes.

Even as it is, I sometimes wonder how the trout get through the winters and find enough to eat up there. The lake is poor habitat for aquatic insects—you'll see scattered midges and the odd Callibaetis mayfly, but that's about it—and it's at an altitude where it's fed almost directly by snowfields, so the growing season is short and the water is stinging cold, even in high summer. But on a good day you can catch some eight- to twelve-inch cutthroats and maybe a few fat, unlikely fifteen- or sixteen-inchers.

You have to hunt your trout here, and the way to do that is to think about how hard their lives are. Sometimes you'll see a loose pod of fish cruising impatiently in open water. They'll take a close look at anything floating on the surface—a windblown seed husk, a sliver of spruce needle, a shred of pinecone—because they can't afford to pass up even an outside chance at food. You don't have to watch for too long to see a fish pick up some inedible piece of bark, ponder it for a few seconds, and then spit it out. After that, it's not much of a stretch to think he might eat your fly, even if it's not perfectly tied.

Most days they'll take almost any dry fly in a size 16 or 18 as long as they're not spooked by the cast, but you have to throw far ahead of the fish: ten or fifteen feet in smooth water, closer if there's a little chop. If they turn away before they get to the fly, you can sometimes give it a gentle twitch and one or two will peel off and come for it. Competition for food is stiff, so if there's more than one trout, the biggest one usually gets there first.

Current is always good, and there are two inlets, a big one and a smaller one, and a nice slow-running channel at the outlet above the logjam. Now and then you'll spot a fish holding in a current tongue, but usually they're working side to side up the current and then falling back, covering water.

At the head of the larger inlet there's a deep plunge pool shrouded in brush that usually holds a good trout, although every now and then he's not there and you can't imagine why. Maybe someone caught him and ate him, maybe he died of old age, or maybe he *is* there, but you spooked him when you tried to snake a cast up under the bush and slapped the water a little too hard.

Sometimes a trout will tuck himself back in the logjam. He'll take your fly if you can drift it in close enough without getting it stuck, but he'll eat it just as it rides up on that little curl where the current piles against the log and then he'll flash back into the sticks. You'll probably lose him in there, even if he's not very big.

Sometimes you'll find good bank feeders; single fish, usually good-sized ones, moving slowly along in the shallows, sometimes just inches from the bank in water so skinny their dorsal fins cut the surface. They're probably looking for ants, beetles, or windblown cripples. These fish can be harder to spot than you'd think, and it's way too easy to creep down to the water's edge and all but step on one.

I remember a great fish from a few seasons ago. I was standing right at the shore, with just my feet in the lake. I'd made a nice long cast out to open water when I glanced to my right and saw a fat, broad-shouldered cutthroat coming up the bank toward me. He was in a few inches of water only a few inches from dry land, and he was so close when I saw him that all I could do was freeze. He swam past me so close he had to edge around the toes of my boots.

I let him get almost out of sight down the bank, then I quietly stepped back into the trees and trotted down the shore to get ahead of him. But I guessed the distance wrong, so when I crept back down to the water, he spooked from right under my feet. He flashed thirty feet out into open water and hung there, wondering what had just almost happened to him. I figured, What the hell? I cast the dry fly four feet to his left, and he swam over and calmly ate it. He was just a hair under sixteen inches long: about as big and wise as he was ever going to get.

That's how wild cutthroats are: They're geniuses in some ways and dumb as posts in others. Their one side helps them survive, and their other side kills them easily. They're so much like us we could be related.

We fished through the afternoon and caught a handful of trout, including a few of the good-sized ones. You don't always see the bigger fish, and I was glad they'd turned up this time. When you finally decide to show someone a spot, you want it to show off a little.

Then we sat on the bank for a while eating a bag of fabulous trail mix I'd brought back from Canada. It had nuts and dried fruit and some macrobiotic-looking green stuff neither of us could identify. The clean, clear air and exercise surely helped, but the stuff really was almost supernaturally delicious, and eating it was a pure animal pleasure.

I guess I just wanted to see the place again for myself, but this time I also wanted to show it to someone who I thought would appreciate it. All fishermen get secretive, but then we begin to be tempted by generosity in a gnawing, guilty sort of way. It had been fun watching the guy's face fall a little when he saw the lake because it didn't look fishy, and then seeing the light dawn. Maybe it was just a weak moment, but he fished it well, liked it a lot, and I felt like I'd done the right thing.

On that trip to British Columbia, less than two weeks earlier,

Vince and I had hiked into an obscure little cutthroat stream with our guide, Dave Campbell. It was small, choked here and there with logjams, and there were some long, fishless, ankle-deep riffles that didn't look like much. But then every hundred yards or so there'd be a deep green pool that seemed to hold one or two big west slope cutthroat trout. By big I mean anywhere from sixteen to twenty inches and heavy for their size. There must be some smaller fish, but you don't see them.

It was different in most ways from the little lake back in Colorado, but it still reminded me of it, and the secrecy surrounding that little creek, and some others like it in the area, is worse than anything I've perpetrated myself back home.

I'd been in this country before, and I'd noticed that the guides will sometimes mix up the names of the creeks, so if you were to get a map and come back on your own you could get confused and never quite find the same stream again. And I have to say that Vince and I were sworn to silence with such solemnity that you can't even be sure I've placed this thing in the right Canadian province.

I understood completely. The little stream was as delicate and perfect as a blown-glass swan, and a competent poacher could clean it out in a week. Halfway through the day I was thinking, It'd be a shame if anyone else knew about this. And then I had to admit, Hell, it's a shame *we* know about it.

I feel the same way about the little lake in Colorado. Virtually undisturbed places aren't common—not here at home, not in Canada, possibly not anywhere—and in the years I've been fishing this thing, I've seen some of our local fisheries get pounded into pale shadows of their former selves. (And yes, I've done my share of the pounding.) I believe there are still undisturbed, if not actually unknown, places, and I still spend some time looking for them, but I realize there is not an endless supply.

That's probably the real difference between being in my twenties and being in my fifties. It's not that I thought I'd live forever back then (they say that about young people, but it's not true), and it's not that I thought things would never change. I just didn't know how or when they'd change, or that once they did, they'd never change back.

Chapter 10

It couldn't have been more than a few days after I hiked into that cutthroat lake that a fisherman I know asked me about a remote stretch of a local stream. He didn't have the right map with him, but he described it by the landmarks, and I knew exactly where he meant.

"Ever fish in there?" he asked.

I automatically said, "You bet."

"So, what's it like?"

After thinking about it for a minute I had to say, "You know, it's been quite a few years, and I don't *remember* what it's like."

He nodded wisely. He's no spring chicken himself.

The fact is, since I've lived in this area, I've fished virtually all of the local drainage—or if I haven't actually cast a fly to every pool and riffle, I've at least hiked along all of it carrying a fly rod. It was the kind of thing you set out to do in your twenties, when you're young and strong with time on your hands and you know you *can* do it.

Maybe I was trying to prove a point or maybe I just wanted to see a large piece of countryside just because it was there, but it must have been important at the time because it was a big project. There are over a hundred miles of fishable stream in the three main forks of the creek, from an arbitrary point above the last town of any size, up the forks to the headwaters near tree line in a national forest, a wilderness area, and a national park.

Exploring all of it took me the better part of two decades. I didn't do it systematically or mark it all off on the maps, and some of those years were between the times I kept a journal, so maybe I missed an odd corner here or there, but I don't think so.

Whatever I set out to prove (and whether or not I actually proved it), fishing all that water was a worthwhile thing to do. Before I was done I'd seen a tremendous amount of beautiful, wild, mostly vacant, mostly public land, I'd caught lots of rainbows, browns, brookies, and cutthroats, and learned either everything I now know about fly-fishing or at least everything I still think is *worth* knowing.

I've talked to plenty of people my age (mid-fifties) who would make a big, half-joking deal about not being able to remember a particular stretch of stream, and I'd started doing that kind of thing myself until no less an authority than my mother corrected me. She said my memory was as good as it ever was. Well, what she actually said was, "You couldn't remember anything when you were sixteen, either," but that would amount to the same thing, right?

But it did make me think I should go back to some of the places I'd forgotten. I wasn't worried about no longer being able to say that I know the drainage like the back of my hand—I will always say that because it's fun to say and damn near impossible to disprove. I was just curious, and curiosity is as good a reason as any to go fishing.

So that summer, I spent the better part of six weeks with a loaded day pack and a rod case leaning next to the back door, ready to go. I rotated three favorite light bamboo rods: a 7½-foot Legacy made by John Bradford, a 7-foot, 9-inch rod made by Mike Clark, and an old 7½-foot F. E. Thomas Special, circa 1940—all two-piece, 5-weights. Some days I was out the door without a thought; other days I could spend half an hour deciding which of those three rods to use. You have to understand that to a bamboo nut, the rod a fish is caught on can be more important than the fish itself.

I spent some full days doing longer hikes, usually with friends, but more often I worked at home in the mornings and went fishing after lunch, when the day turned hot and wading in an ice-cold trout stream started to sound pretty good; fishing within a half-hour or forty-five-minute drive from home. It was an ominously hot summer, with a record number of days ninety degrees and above, so standing in cold water wasn't just an idle thought.

It occurred to me that if everyone who wanted to could work half days and fish the other half, life would be much better, although it's more likely that the people who didn't want to do that would end up ruling the world.

On most of these trips I went light. I waded wet and took the fly rod, a small day pack with odds and ends, and a single fly box. I hauled more gear than that when I first started fishing here. Years ago I usually suffered long hikes with waders—either wearing them or carrying them—and I always wore a vest, even though I didn't need all the pockets, because a fisherman was just supposed to wear a vest to look properly hip. (The sport hadn't hit its full pace yet, but it was already a fashion statement.)

Now, when I'm hiking back out in shorts with a small pack on my back, I'm liable to break down the rod and carry it casually close to my leg, trying to look as little like a fisherman as possible. That way, if I meet someone on the trail, maybe I can avoid answering those impertinent questions like "Where were you fishing?" and "Did you get any?" and "How big were they?" I have always been as secretive and uncharitable as you'd expect from someone with the gall to claim a hundred miles of stream as his home water.

When I started fishing the East Slope of the Colorado Rockies in my twenties, fly-fishing was nowhere near as popular as it is now and the state's population was a lot smaller. There weren't as many fly fishers around, and many of the ones who were here were older guys who often didn't hike as far as my friends and I did. At the time I thought they couldn't do it anymore. Now—with a little more perspective—I think most of them were capable of it; they just didn't feel like it.

Virtually all the really good streams—good at least in terms of size and numbers of fish—were well known, but with a little effort and a topographic map, you could get on streams that were seldom fished and have as much of them as you liked all to yourself.

That's easier in some places than in others, but you can still do it. It's just that now you have to study the map more closely and walk farther. It seems a little unfair that now that I'm older I have to make longer hikes to find these places, but it keeps me in shape, and I guess it's not the worst injustice life can hand out.

I also spent quite a few afternoons driving the fifteen or twenty miles of road that roughly parallel one of the forks of the creek and just stopping at the turnouts where I could no longer quite remember what the stream looked like. (Over time you develop your favorite spots, but you have to wonder if you've really cherry picked the best water or just fallen into a rut.) I'd either fish upstream or hike down a quarter- to a half-mile and work my way back to the truck. In this way I spent some very pleasant days and covered a lot of water, often alone, sometimes with Mike Price.

This whole stretch is in a narrow canyon, and the water is steep, fast, and choked with pockets, boulders, and logjams. Except for a few distinctive pools, one mile of it looks very much like another. It's also the kind of stream you can't leapfrog very easily, so when there are two fishermen, you trade pools, with one guy fishing and the other making wisecracks. It takes two people who are good friends and who aren't greedy or impatient.

Mike has lived here all his life and was almost literally born on the banks of this stream. He's fished it for much longer than I have—over forty years now—so he has the distinction of having forgotten some of this stuff twice to my once. Still, one or both of us would almost always end up saying, "Yeah, now that I get down here, I remember this. I remember those rocks and this pool, but that big log didn't used to be there."

This is mostly all wild brown trout water now, shading into brookies as you get up near the head of the canyon. The way brown trout are with weather, it naturally fishes better on cloudy days, but the canyon is steep and twisty, so you can almost always find a shady patch where the fish are looking up.

Mike remembers cutthroats through here, but except for the odd holdout, those were mostly gone from this stretch by the time I came along. They'd either been fished out or out-competed by the stocked rainbows and browns. The rainbows are pretty much gone now, too, ever since the Division of Wildlife stopped stocking them because of problems with whirling disease, and that has let the browns come back nicely. They're fat and healthy, and you'll see them in all sizes, from dinks too small to eat a size 16 dry fly all the way up to a few old boys fourteen and fifteen inches long.

The browns were introduced, but they've been here for so long that even the oldest locals don't remember when they *stopped* stocking them, let alone when they started.

There are more fishermen now—though nothing like the crowds you see on tailwaters—and in some of the easier spots they've taken a toll. But, as always, if you're willing to scramble over boulders the size of pickup trucks or hike a few miles, you'll do fine. And there are lots of boulders; lots of miles to hike.

So, is the fishing better or worse here than it was twenty, or for that matter, forty years ago? Mike and I have talked about that, and we agree it's hard to say for sure when you're fishing in part to refresh faded memories.

The thing is, if you leave a piece of water alone long enough, either it changes or you forget what it was like. Either way, it's as if you never fished it before. It's a nice thought that there's more water in your own neighborhood than you can wrap your mind around, and in the end it becomes that chance they say you never get: the one where you can go back and do something again for the first time.

When I first moved west, I spent a lot more time than I do now on those small roadside creeks: the one that eventually became my home water and some others, too. They were quick and easy to get to (especially after work), they were seldom if ever crowded, they were a manageable size for an inexperienced wader and caster, and no one had yet bothered to tell me I was supposed to want something better.

These creeks are all over the place in the Rocky Mountains, and for a while after I moved here in the late '60s, I shared the common misconception of newcomers that this was wet country. "Seems like everywhere I go there's a stream," people would say, which was true enough if they went everywhere in a car.

But then a professor of fisheries biology explained to me that much of the West is actually semiarid. "You see lots of water in the mountains and foothills," he said, "because stream canyons were the only places where the roads could be built. But everyplace else is dry as a bone."

He was right. It seemed like every little mountain road I drove on, whether it was paved or dirt, two wheel- or four-wheel-drive, went along a creek because—once you thought about it—it couldn't possibly go anywhere else. If you picked your routes carefully, you could drive hundreds of miles through the mountains and foothills and rarely be out of sight of a stream with trout in it. Life in the West was starting to look pretty good.

Naturally, some of these are good-sized, well-known, hard-fished rivers, but many more of them are small and insignificant-looking. They flow beside roads that don't seem to go anywhere special, they don't have reputations—either good or bad—and you won't be able to track many of their courses or even find some of their names except on the most detailed maps. They're tributaries of tributaries: the east fork of the north branch of the something-or-other. They're usually steep, undammed freestones that depend on snowmelt for their water, so they roar in the spring, trickle in the fall, freeze in the winter, and otherwise do what streams have always done. And it has never ceased to amaze me how many of them are full of trout.

How the fish got there can be a mystery unless you want to do a lot of nit-picking research, and sometimes even that won't help. A good deal of the early stocking in the Rockies was done haphazardly and anonymously, either with or without the blessing of wildlife officials, so some records are long buried and others never existed in the first place.

In some of these creeks the trout were once planted where you'll still find them, but in others the fish worked their way upstream from larger rivers or downstream from lakes and reservoirs. They might be brook trout, brown trout, rainbows, or a mix. Now and then you'll find cutthroats, though more likely they'll be rainbow-cutthroat hybrids.

It's always a kick to get a so-called native trout, but the fact is, even the pure cutts usually turn out to be the results of reintroductions or early plantings that, for instance, put Yellowstone cutthroats into the Platte River drainage that used to hold greenbacks. (That was a mistake by modern standards, but at the time it seemed like a good idea.)

Whatever they are and however they got there, they're the kind of trout that fate put in the stream, they're only as big as they're supposed to be, and by now, generations of fish later, many of them have gone ragged-ass wild and are part of the landscape. If they lack any romance at all, it's our fault, not theirs.

Naturally, some of these creeks are in better shape than others. Sometimes a stream next to a road was channelized during construction into one big riffle that has great bug habitat, but no holding water for fish. In the worst of these you can see the former trout habitat bulldozed into neat piles on the banks. But then others seem weirdly untouched, as if the road builders took great pains not to disturb them—as hard as that is to picture. Now and then, especially in steep canyons, some of the sloppy riprap along the road has tumbled into the creek to make fishy pools, glides, and pockets that weren't there before. For every creek that was wrecked by road construction, there's another that was either left untouched or made a little better. In the long run, it probably evens out.

A lot of fishermen ignore these small creeks by the sides of roads because most of us seem to want to fish in water that's either big-ger and better known or more remote, and that's understandable, since most of our idealized mental pictures of fly-fishing in the West don't include even light traffic. But the fact is, some of the smaller roadside streams are so overlooked that they're much less crowded and effectively wilder than water you'll go a lot farther to fish.

The roads eventually turn or stop (thank God), and the creeks snake on off into the mountains. It's tempting to go on from there on foot for all kinds of reasons, but there have been days when I hiked miles into a wilderness area or national park and saw more fishermen than if I'd pulled over on the canyon road twenty miles back and fished next to the truck.

Sometimes you can find these little streams listed in guidebooks, but I think the descriptions are often based on hearsay twice removed, because they're likely to be wrong about the things that count, like species of fish and average size. And of course the listings don't change from one edition to the next, but the streams do. You'll get bigger, fatter trout after a few high-water years and smaller ones after a dry season or two. The places where one species of trout begins to shade into another will also move around, some-times by miles.

Now and then you can get advice from a local fisherman about a neglected roadside creek, but don't count on it being accurate. As we all know, it is considered honorable to lie to protect a secret fishing spot, and after looking at some of these little things it's easy to believe someone who shrugs and says, "Oh, it might have a cou-ple a' little brookies in it, but that's about it."

I've fished a fair number of roadside creeks around the West over the years, and I've admired many more from a car window on my way to fish somewhere else. I've also come close to wrecking my pickup a few times because I was watching the creek instead of where I was going. Imagine a narrow, winding road, a trout rising in a lovely little pool, and a UPS truck in the oncoming lane. Luckily, my friends and I have developed an ass-backwards system whereby the driver watches the stream and the passenger watches the road. Conversations degenerate into shorthand. One guy says, "Rise." The other says, "Heads up!"

I've never been methodical about it, but sometimes, after driving along a creek off and on for years without ever seeing anyone fishing it or hearing much about it, I finally can't stand it anymore. The only way to know about the thing is to string up a rod and fish it— and suddenly not knowing about it has become unbearable.

A lot of them turned out to be what most fishermen assume they are: small, skinny, rugged, hard to fish, hard to get around in, with pretty wild trout no bigger than about eight or nine inches long. I enjoy fishing those because they take me back to when fly-fishing allowed for a little homespun subsistence. In those days there were basically three kinds of trout: dinks, which were plentiful; hogs, which were caught mostly in exotic places by magazine writers; and keepers. A nine-inch trout is on the short end of being a keeper, and lots of meals of three or four small trout and a big pile of fried potatoes could help you to work cheap and fish hard.

Fly-fishing can be upscale and exotic if you want it to be and can afford that, but at base it's homegrown, backyard stuff: something people used to do when the chores were done; a way of goofing off that was just barely justified by a couple of fresh fish for supper. It seems important to remember that for most of the sport's long history, anyone who spent hundreds of dollars on a fly rod and released all the fish they caught would have been run out of town.

But then some of the creeks I've taken the time to explore thoroughly have been surprisingly good. Usually these are streams fairly close to home, and even at that, it's taken me a day here and a day there over a season or two to have a proper look around. Still, if I go to enough trouble, there probably will be a couple of stretches of unusually good water. Maybe it's a series of steep plunge pools with nearly impassable boulder piles for banks, like some of the water Mike and I had been fishing; or pocket water so crowded with brush that your fly spends more time in the bushes than in the creek. It might also be an ordinary piece of water where the turnouts on the road happen to be three miles apart and no one in the last few years has felt like walking that far on a nothing little creek on the way to someplace better.

I want to think that the best water is always the hardest to get to and fish—and it works out that way often enough—but I've also been surprised over the last few seasons at how many nice trout I've caught right through campgrounds, whether they're those big, pay-to-camp jobs in the national forest or just gravel turnouts with a picnic table. I always thought the wide trails pounded down to the creeks at these spots meant that they'd been fished out, but apparently that's not always the case.

Maybe people fish there, but they don't fish well. (I once found a six-inch-long Rapala lure hung on the bottom of a creek where the biggest trout you could expect to catch would only be two inches longer than that.) Or maybe the trails are made by picnickers and sight-seers. We fishermen sometimes forget that normal people are drawn to streams, too. Whatever the reason, I've come to think of this as the Campground Syndrome: People assume it's fished out, so hardly anyone fishes there. Consequently, it's full of fish.

Wherever the good water turns out to be, you're suddenly into some comparatively big trout—thirteen, maybe even fourteen inches long—and after launching baby fish from the water on a light rod for the last few hours, you'll probably break the first one off.

Sometimes it's just that one trout and it's a heartbreaker, but more often there's a hundred yards or a quarter mile of water where the trout are fewer but bigger, and it's like you're suddenly on a different stream. In a sport where a fourteen-inch trout is no longer much to brag about, you are suddenly happier than you can remember being for a long time.

And it's more or less right there by the side of the road. You can probably see a car go by now and then. If not, you can probably hear one if you stop and listen, although the *shoosh* of a passing car can blend so well with the sound of current it can be hard to pick out. You've stumbled upon something fine that no one else seems to have noticed, and you begin to worry that your pickup parked up there on the side of the road could give it away.

This reminds me of that feeling you had as a kid, back before the angst and the hormones kicked in. You remember: You were always finding neat stuff the big people overlooked because they were in too much of a hurry; overhearing things because they thought you weren't paying attention. You and the dog were the only ones in the house who knew what was behind the couch.

These little creeks are perfect for beginning fly fishers because they're so forgiving, and they're great to come back to years later for the same reason. Sometimes when I get home from a long, expensive trip for big fish, I'll get into a bout of post-trip depression. I'll mope around, refuse to read my mail, or listen to the answering machine, maybe do the worst of the dirty laundry but otherwise keep stubbornly living out of the duffel bag for a few more days.

I don't understand why it happens, because I'm usually ready to come home after most trips. After all, it's in the nature of these things to end: It's the difference between going on a trip to Canada and moving there. I suppose I'll never put my finger on the exact cause without actually going through therapy, although in a general way, not being quite ready to come home from a great fishing trip is no mystery.

For some people—those who spoil easily—fish size is the single cause of the depression they feel after a trip to some exotic place. I've actually heard a few fishermen come right out and say it: Once they'd caught the big bruisers in Canada, Alaska, or wherever, they just couldn't enjoy the smaller fish in their home waters anymore.

Some of those guys were clearly posturing, but a few actually seemed to mean it, and all I could think was, You poor bastard. Of course, I shouldn't be that smug, because over time I've been prone to almost every known human failing, but so far—through luck or some hidden strength of character—catching the occasional big fish hasn't ruined me. And at this late date there's a pretty good chance it never will.

So after a day or two of being a self-absorbed pain in the ass, I'll go to some roadside creek, catch a few little trout, and realize I'm back and I'm okay. It might occur to me that the pigs I was catching just last week could, and would, eat these things for lunch, but it's no more than an observation.

When you finally do stumble on a sweet little piece of water by the side of the road that no one else seems to have found, you can feel like it's yours alone, but it's not. Fishermen flock to the latest hot spots like everyone else, but deep down we're a nosy, inquisitive breed, and for any seemingly insignificant little roadside creek there are a few locals who know it well and some travelers who at least stop at the obvious turnouts and wet a line out of curiosity.

I've always liked people who will happily fish any old half-baked stream just to see what's in it, although I'm not always any happier to see them on the water than they are to see me. Sometimes when two fishermen have both discovered something that's under the radar of most other anglers, they'll exchange that wave that's polite enough but still somehow manages to say "you son of a bitch."

But there's a kind of absurdity to all this that keeps it from ever getting too serious. I mean, here are two strangers with fly rods, both wondering which of them is the intruder, and both desperate to keep a secret no one really wants to know.

CHAPTER 11

We were on a road trip through Wyoming to fish some roadside creeks farther from home when Mike Price and I stopped at a fly shop in Cody to see Mike's friend Johnny. As we drove down into town in Mike's big blue Suburban packed to the windows with fishing tackle and camping gear, Mike said, "You'll enjoy this," which didn't tell me much. Mike has an off-center sense of fun, so coming from him, that could have meant anything from free coffee to the possibility of a fistfight.

Johnny turned out to be a small, lean, slow-talking local cowboy with a large mustache and a prickly sense of humor who's fished the area all his life: the kind of guy you used to meet all the time in Western fishing joints in the days before everyone in the business suddenly got so young and clean-cut. He remembered Mike and didn't seem horrified to see him, which I took as a good sign.

This was a real social call, but we were also hoping for a little information. When he'd first met Johnny, Mike had been traveling with his girlfriend (now wife), Sandy. He thought Johnny might have been a little charmed by her—a real possibility—because he'd been surprisingly free with leads on places to fish.

I said, "So you're hoping some of Sandy's charm rubbed off on you?"

"Yeah," Mike said, as if that made perfect sense.

I said, "Well, don't count on it."

We'd been camping and fishing in the Bighorn Mountains for the last few days, and now we were on our way to an obscure brook trout creek that Mike knows about somewhere off the eastern boundary of Yellowstone Park. It's one of those places where few fishermen ever go because it's mostly unknown, but even if it wasn't, some would think it's too long a drive and too hard a hike for fish that are fat, beautiful, and dumb but not all that big.

Anyway, we wanted to find out what kind of shape the creek was in, because it had been raining off and on for three days and this was the kind of water that could muddy up easily.

Johnny said it might well be off-color the way the weather had been, but he hadn't been up there recently himself and he didn't know anyone who had. He made a few phone calls but couldn't reach anyone. Apparently there aren't many people with telephones near the creek, although Johnny seemed to have all their numbers memorized.

"I don't know what to tell you," Johnny said, making it clear that whatever we decided to do, it was out of his hands.

Mike and I agreed to bag that and go somewhere else. It would have been a three-hour drive on increasingly bad roads—a long way to go to gamble on a muddy stream. And this was also an area known for its grizzly bears. In fact, the landmark where you begin the long hike in is the DANGER GRIZZLY BEARS sign, and more than one local had advised us to carry side arms in there. After Mike's stories about the place, I'd been eager to go and I wasn't particularly scared, but I noticed a little surge of relief when we called it off.

After all, this was the kind of trip where you'd expect to run into a grizzly. So far we'd nearly hit a black bear on the road, had a storm one night that all but blew down the camp, and been chased out of two pools on the North Tongue, one by a cow moose with a calf and one by a skinny, nasty little range cow, also with a calf.

We got out our maps, and Johnny pointed out a few streams, some of which we'd already fished. He was pretty free with the more obvious places, but when it came to the little hidden sweet spots, he'd just tap the place on the map with his finger and look meaningfully into our eyes, as if by not actually speaking the name of the stream, he wouldn't really be giving anything away.

We thanked him and drove to the spot he'd tapped the hardest while giving us what we thought was the most meaningful look. Given the circumstances, I feel free to say only that it was a good fifty miles from the nearest town with a stoplight and, what with unmarked roads and our mediocre map, it took us a while to find it.

There was a small, cottonwood-shaded campground—almost empty—a sandstone cliff covered with, according to the local ranger, eleven thousand years' worth of Native American petroglyphs, and a pretty little trout stream flowing southwest out of some arid-looking canyon lands. According to the map, the stream above the campground had no road access for the rest of its course, a distance of maybe thirty miles.

It was the middle of a hot, sunny afternoon without a breath of wind, but Mike and I had been on the road since we broke camp early that morning and didn't feel like waiting for it to cool down.

When we started up the creek, we met an elderly fisherman just coming out. He had an automatic reel on a fiberglass fly rod—one of those old brown ones that was made to resemble bamboo—and he was carrying three dead brown trout.

Mike said, "What are they biting on?"

The guy said, "Well, I tried worms, but what they wanted was hoppers. It was harder catching the damn bait than it was catching the fish." I remembered that from my bait fishing days: Hoppers are best picked like berries in the cool of the morning. Once they get warm, they're way too fast and agile.

He said he hadn't gone far because the banks were thickly overgrown. "Back in the old days," he said, "Old What's-his-name used to graze his cows up here, and there were trails all along the creek. Now the damn state's got it for winter elk range and the trails are all grown over. Hell, to go very far up there now a guy'd have to walk right in the stream."

So Mike and I hiked up until a guy'd have to walk right in the stream to go any farther and fished on from there. The old man was right: The banks were a god-awful tangle of willow, cottonwood, dogwood, clematis, and poison ivy, all growing up through a litter of deadfall. I couldn't imagine how he'd managed to chase grasshoppers through this stuff without breaking a leg.

This was a long, narrow valley with not much tilt to it. It was thick and green as a jungle along the water, bare and deserty on the hillsides, with a blue sky framed in pink rim rock. Sometimes the stream ran for a long way in thin riffles, but at every bend was a big, deep pool with a few trout.

It was hot, still, and quiet up there, without a sign of people. We saw hawks and eagles, a big mule deer, and once a large, crumbling black bear track in the sand.

I was fishing a #14 Whitlock Hopper, and I think Mike had on a size 12 yellow Stimulator. The first few browns we caught were fat and healthy and about eight or nine inches long—the same size fish the old man had on his stringer—but as we worked our way up the stream, the fish gradually got bigger. In fact, we decided later that the trout got another inch longer on average for every three or four pools. They were like the lines on a ruler measuring the distance from the campground and the difficulty of the hike. By the time we got far enough in there to have to turn around to make it out by dark, the biggest trout were pushing fifteen inches.

Before we started back, we both stood and gazed upstream for a while. We'd gone maybe two miles, tops, and the trout had gotten steadily bigger the whole way. There were at least twenty-eight more roadless miles of this thing to go, and you have to think . . . Well, you know.

This had been a long, hard hike on a brutally hot day. We were tired, drenched with sweat, and dehydrated, so when we got back we each drank a quart of water too quickly and got headaches. Then we stripped naked and jumped in the cold stream. That stopped my heart briefly, and I'm sure it wasn't pretty, either, but it sure felt good.

After we set up camp and cooked supper, Mike volunteered to wash the dishes and I walked over to look at the petroglyphs again. We'd given them only an impatient five minutes on the way in because we were anxious to fish. There was just enough light left to see them and the two or three people who had been looking at them earlier were gone, so I had them to myself in the last good light.

There were animals (snakes, mule deer, something that might have been an antelope) and either spirit people with round bodies and horns or humans in headdresses behind shields. Some were holding spears. Others seemed to have spears going through them, as did some of the animals. I sketched some of the stranger ones in my journal. I'm no Muriel Foster, and I didn't begin to do them justice, but I thought maybe I'd look them up later to see what some anthropologist had guessed about them.

The overall effect of the cliff was that of a Picasso mural, and my uneducated suspicion is that its purpose was roughly the same; there would be imponderable layers of tradition and meaning, but in the end it was just something some people were moved to do for their own reasons and that some other people were moved to look at. And it was in a place that would allow for enough leisure to do the work and then stand back to appreciate it.

This was the kind of perfect spot a traveler can stumble on now and then. The mouth of the canyon was wide and lush with underbrush and stands of tall, straight narrow-leaf cottonwoods that had reached up out of the canyon to put their crowns in the sunlight. The trees were draped so thickly in wild clematis vines that on some you could no longer see the trunks, and the vines themselves were alive with orioles, tanagers, and warblers. The cliffs and trees made shelter from the wind and shade from the sun. There was good water, game, berries, medicinal herbs, firewood, trout: everything you'd need. For at least the last one hundred ten centuries, this had been a good place to camp.

Native Americans passed through there for thousands of years, apparently staying for long periods of time. Later, cattle were grazed there and eventually a ranch took hold, even though up until then the concept of ownership had been unknown here. Now, as the old man had said, the "damn state has it." The ranger and his family live in the old ranch house. It would be the perfect job if you enjoyed doing for yourself and didn't need a lot of noise or company.

On the same cliff with the petroglyphs were the painted names of some turn-of-the-century cowboys. If you put your name on this cliff now you'd be shot—and rightfully so—but the archeologists apparently decided to leave the old cowpoke graffiti for historical reasons. The names and dates were off to the side, not painted over the old stuff or even very close to it. Maybe it wasn't vandalism. Maybe it was just someone saying, "Yeah, we were here, too." I have to say it seemed fairly respectful.

But then no one was ever shown less respect than the native tribes who were systematically wiped out for no other reason than that they were bad for business. (They didn't teach it like that when I was in school, but I understand they're starting to now. I suppose it amounts to a small step forward.) Then later, archeologists came along and desecrated their grandparents' graves. They probably didn't mean it to be the final insult, but that's what it was. I love this old rock art and have now and then traveled far out of my way to see it, but I can never look at it with a completely clear conscience.

I sat there until it was full dark and the bats and nighthawks were out, having a nice enough time but stopping short of having the mystical experience I'd have once thought was required under the circumstances. I *am* a religious man in a nonspecific, nonpracticing sort of way. That is, I think the religious impulse is one of the finest things about the human race, but that organized religion can be one of the worst. As for other peoples' religions, I agree with Jim Harrison, who said, "You cannot greedily suck out of another culture what you have failed to find in your own heart."

I waited until I figured Mike was good and done with the dishes and then walked back to camp.

The next day was another hot one: already pushing ninety degrees by the time we finished breakfast. We wanted to go farther up the little stream, but it would have been a brutal walk, and it probably would have gotten hot enough to put the fishing off for most of the day. Still, it was tempting. The brown trout had gone from about eight to fourteen or fifteen inches in two miles of stream. We knew that wouldn't go on forever, but we also didn't know where it would stop. At sixteen inches? At eighteen? Not likely in water like this, but conceivable.

Or, better yet, maybe we could go far enough to start getting into some cutthroats. Before the browns were introduced here God knows how many years ago, this would have been cutthroat water if there were any fish at all. Maybe way back up in there, some of the old trout were still holding out. There's probably a fisheries biologist somewhere who knows all about that, but possibly not. Even now, there are odd corners of the West that have been overlooked, and it's an outright kick in the ass to find one.

If I know my native trout, they'd be Fine-spotted Snake River Cutthroats, although I've been wrong about that kind of thing before. Whatever they were, once you found them they'd be easy to get. As M. R. Montgomery said, "Anytime it's hard to catch trout, you are not in the real West."

We talked it over. We could each chug a gallon of water to prehydrate and put in four or five miles before we wet a line. Or we could pack in a light camp, eat a few trout, drink boiled stream water, and stay overnight. Maybe two nights. If we were up to it— and if it wasn't so damned hot—maybe we could get farther up there than anyone had gone in a year or two. An easy thought while you're sitting in the shade drinking coffee.

In the end we packed up and headed back into the mountains, where we knew it would be cool and the fish would be biting. There was a pang of regret that's there to this day, but it still seemed like the best thing to do. We promised each other that we'd come back there and do it in September or early October when the weather would be cooler and the fishing would be good all day, but we didn't.

CHAPTER 12

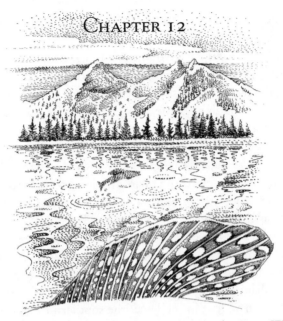

I don't remember exactly how long that road trip to Wyoming lasted, but it was a good long one, and that's rare because Mike and I don't always get to fish together as much as we'd like. That's mostly because of his job. He works at a nearby cement plant, where he has a strange schedule that I can't keep track of: odd hours, odd days on and off. He also now and then vanishes into several weeks of night shifts and becomes nocturnal for a while. And although I don't completely understand what he does at the plant, he's valuable enough that when something goes wrong, he has to be there to fix it, whether it's his day off or not.

In fact, Mike fits Tom McGuane's definition of a "real fisherman" as someone who works hard at a regular job and then fishes just as hard when he's off. There are mornings when we met for breakfast at a cafe before heading out to fish somewhere. I'll be fresh from a good night's sleep, and Mike will have been off the graveyard shift just long enough to take a shower and grab his gear.

He'll be tired but eager (you wouldn't notice the tiredness if you didn't know him), and later that day I might find him sleeping, although never when the fishing is good. If things slow down and I lose track of him, he's easy to locate by the snoring. It sounds like a raccoon eating a live chicken.

Anyway, Mike and I were out in my fourteen-foot john boat on a grayling lake up near Cameron Pass in northern Colorado. We'd put in on the north side, just off the access road: a clumsy operation because, even though boats are allowed on this lake, the Forest Service, in its infinite wisdom, keeps the gate at the boat ramp closed and padlocked.

The wind was up and there was a low white chop on the water, so we immediately rowed the quarter mile or so over to the south shore. That's where the glassy water was and that's what grayling like. Years ago a guide in the Northwest Territories told me that grayling were lazy fish because they'll rise only in slow currents in rivers and smooth water in lakes. Like most rules of thumb in fishing, that's only about half right, but then it's also only half wrong.

It was a haul rowing against a stiff head wind in a box-shaped boat, but when we got in the lee of the southern ridge we found a pod of fish rising to midges in a sheltered cove. I took the oars while Mike cast. He got a fish or two, but in a few minutes the wind switched around out of the northwest, a chop came up on the water, and the fish stopped rising.

A nymph would have worked—grayling don't actually go away when the water gets rough, they just stop rising because they have trouble seeing the bugs—but they're such a perfect dry fly fish it's sort of a shame to go underwater for them.

From out on the lake, we could see one ominous gray thunderstorm directly to our west, oozing up over the Continental Divide, and another one several miles off to the northwest, with ragged white clouds scudding across the rest of an otherwise brilliant blue sky. The sun was warm when it was out, but the wind had the kind of cold bite you can feel through the weave of a wool sweater. This is what passes for summertime in the range known as the Never Summer Mountains.

There was now a nice strip of glassy water along the north shore—the one we'd just come from—but we were too far away to see if there were any rising fish. And anyway, this was shaping up as the kind of unsettled day when the wind direction would change every twenty minutes, so even if the fish were coming up, it probably wouldn't last long. I said to Mike, "I'm not gonna get sucked into rowing back and forth across this thing for the next eight hours."

We could see that the fishing was going to be a little bit of a struggle, so we set a leisurely pace, working slowly up the lake toward the inlet—sometimes against a head wind—casting dry flies to what calm water we could find and hooking the occasional grayling. Most were small, but there were enough of the better ones to keep our interest up.

Here in Colorado, a good grayling is, say, around eleven to thirteen inches long. You'll now and then see bigger ones, but not many. (The state record that's stood since 1974 is one pound, seven ounces.) In years past I've caught grayling weighing from two to almost three pounds in rivers in Alaska and the Northwest Territories, and they really come into their own at that size, especially on light tackle in a good current. Back home we fish for them because they're strange, rare, and beautiful, not for the size or the fight.

The Arctic grayling isn't a well-known or much-loved game fish in Colorado. In the Division of Wildlife's fishing regulation brochure there's a list of "popular cold-water sport fish" that includes whitefish, but not grayling. Since 1973, grayling have been planted in thirty-six lakes, reservoirs, and a few creeks around the state, but many of those plantings didn't take and the fish can be hard to find unless you do a little research.

Apparently some grayling were also stocked earlier than that—possibly as far back as the 1950s—but I haven't been able to dig up those records. I like to think that somewhere in these mountains there are some undocumented, lost, and pretty much forgotten grayling lakes that a guy could locate through either painstaking research or plain dumb luck.

As far as I can tell, it's the same in the other Western states where grayling have been introduced: There aren't many, and there isn't a lot of excitement about them, but you can find them if you're willing to look. And if you're persistent enough to dig up a fisheries biologist who's into them, you can get your ear chewed off about pitiful budgets and no respect. The wildlife agency in every Western state has a fisheries guy who lies awake at night worrying about grayling while no one else seems to care.

In fact, grayling aren't even supposed to be in the lake we were fishing. They were planted years ago in an alpine lake a few miles above this one where, a couple of decades ago, I caught and ate the first few grayling I ever saw and then watched the Perseid meteor shower in the thin air at eleven thousand feet. As I recall, I had a drink or two and got dizzy.

Later the grayling were poisoned out of that lake to make room for a planting of native cutthroats. But at some point a few of them must have worked their way down a tiny feeder creek and colonized the lake, which in the meantime had been stocked with Emerald Lake rainbows. The grayling are a little overpopulated, so there must not be enough rainbows to keep their numbers down.

We catch one of the rainbows every now and then on a small dry fly—usually a little fish. There are supposed to be some nice ones in there, but we've never gone after them. Might have to try that sometime. A sink-tip line and a silvery gray–colored baby grayling streamer would probably work.

The grayling's original range stretches from the Arctic Circle through most of northern Canada and Alaska, with populations in Montana and, once, Michigan, although the Michigan grayling are long gone now. They were too easy to catch, too good to eat, too sensitive to rivers ruined by logging.

All the grayling in North America are arctic grayling: *Thymallus arcticus.* The Montana grayling is a subspecies: *Thymallus arcticus montanus,* and that's probably what you'll catch now anywhere south of Canada or Alaska. According to John D. Varley and Paul Schullery in *Yellowstone Fishes,* virtually all the grayling now living in the Western U.S. originally came from Montana grayling eggs collected at Grebe Lake in Yellowstone Park.

That same book says that there are no longer "viable populations" of grayling in their native Montana rivers (they're all pretty much lake fish now), although it doesn't seem like that long ago that I caught them in fair numbers in the Madison and the Big Hole. But then maybe it *was* that long ago. You know how it is with time and fishing.

It's never been hard for me to like grayling. They're pretty; out-rageously prehistoric-looking with that high, spotted dorsal fin; not too smart; good to eat if you can bear to kill one; and they have an endearing taste for small dry flies.

They're enthusiastic fish with a tendency to literally pounce on a floating fly. Smaller fish will sometimes jump out of the water next to a fly and land face down on top of it. Bigger ones will take in a half roll. Either way, you can miss strikes because you see the fish before he actually eats the fly, so you set too soon. I'm sure there's a good evolutionary reason for that kind of rise form, but it always looks to me like the fish are playing. Either that, or they're so happy to see a bug, they can't contain themselves.

It also seems to me that grayling sort of fall between the cracks in a sporting sense. Most fisheries managers find them mildly inter-esting. Most fly fishers are curious about them, like them well enough when they catch a few, and like to say they *have* caught them, but they usually won't go far to do it.

In their northern range, grayling usually live in the same water with larger, sexier fish, and the biggest grayling I've caught have been on trips for lake trout, pike, rainbows, char, and salmon. A lot of fishermen up there look at grayling the way bass fishers look at bluegills: They're neat when they're real big, but mostly they're just easy and tasty.

Years ago, at a place called Snowbird Lake Lodge in the North-west Territories, most of the sports and all of the guides had decided my friends and I were nuts after the first few days of fish-ing. The area was known for its big lake trout—a thirty-pounder was considered a nice one—but we spent most of our time catch-ing two- to three-pound grayling on dry flies on the Kazan River. We tried to explain that a three-pound grayling was world-record class, but no one seemed impressed. Fly-fishing had begun to catch on big time back home, but the craze hadn't yet reached that far north, and guys with wussy tackle chasing little fish amounted to comic relief for the Bubbas.

But then disapproval has always been a source of encouragement for me, and it was on that trip that I began to think maybe one way to stay happy as a fisherman was to quietly leave the guided tour and take up with unpopular fish. I'd done the same thing when choosing some of my friends, and that had worked out well enough.

Mike and I caught grayling off and on all afternoon and into the evening between bouts of dodging the weather. The lake is sort of an elongated, bumpy pear shape with a wide bowl and a gradually narrowing channel running up to the inlet. We got up in the channel because that's usually a good spot anyway and because we wanted to be close to one bank or the other when a sudden squall started to raise whitecaps. When you're out on these mountain reservoirs, summer thunderstorms can sneak up from behind nearby peaks and be on you before you can row to shore.

A few times we sucked it up and fished nymphs when the water stayed too rough for too long, and of course they worked. We used the obvious patterns—Hare's Ears and Pheasant Tails in a size 16, lightly weighted—but it didn't really matter. I've never known grayling to be very selective. They do like little flies, but that's only because they have small mouths.

Mike had gotten into grayling only once before, so every time he landed one he'd hold it in the water and admire that huge, iridescent, spotted fin—turning it this way and that in the light to see the colors change—as if he still didn't quite believe it. I've caught lots of them over the years and I did the same thing. Of course, you never want to hold on to a fish for too long because the quicker you get him released, the less chance you have of hurting him, and also because a caught fish will regard you with the kind of level gaze that can be disconcerting. It's as if he's saying, "Well, what now? Death or just a close call?"

That big fin is what grayling are all about. Otherwise they're a plain, fairly drab creature with a small pouty mouth and a few dark spots on the body. They look prehistoric, and you get the feeling that the fish is an appendage of the fin instead of the other way around. A friend once described them as whitefish on LSD.

Grayling have always reminded me of the dinosaur-like early reptile called a dimetrodon that also had a big skin-and-spine sail on its back and that in fact looks like a huge, hideous, flesh-eating grayling with legs. Paleontologists have speculated that the dimetrodon sail was an organ for dissipating heat, but I don't believe it. Clumsy and otherwise useless accessories—from antlers on bull elk to red convertibles on middle-aged guys—always come down to sex.

So it was an ordinary day of fighting wind on a mountain lake—honestly trying to stay within the bounds of boating safety—and catching fish anyway. Twice we were blown off the water and huddled on shore in rain gear until the squalls passed, but mostly we fished nymphs halfheartedly in the wind and switched quickly to dries when the lake glassed off and the fish started to rise.

Nymphs didn't produce bigger grayling the way they sometimes will with trout. In fact, the biggest grayling we got all day came right to the top for dry flies. You've gotta love that.

Along about the middle of the day, Mike casually mentioned that he'd never eaten a grayling. I said I'd eaten some for shore lunch in Canada and they were delicious: mild, white, and flaky; more like Dover sole than any trout. We said we should string a few up for later, but somehow we never got around to it. I'm not sure why. Either we didn't have the heart for it, or we were catching so many fish we figured we could kill a couple anytime, so why bother to do it now? I grew up in an era when fishermen ate fish and, conservation notwithstanding, that still seems perfectly natural. But for some reason I'm now more likely to get sentimental about it than I am to actually do it.

I told Mike what the fisheries biologist had told me about why there were grayling in this lake in the first place. Mike thought that over for a minute and then said that if they'd managed to work their way down that little trickle from the lake above, they had probably also dribbled out the bottom of this lake into the larger stream below.

I'd never thought of that, but of course they had. They'd be down there right now, in that fast pocket water with the browns and rainbows, waiting for any excuse to rise to a dry fly. We added that to the list of things that must be tried the next chance we get. It's a list that grows faster than we can fish, so there's always this widening field of possibilities ahead of us.

By evening we were rowing back across the lake toward the truck, on the down side of a thirty- or forty-fish day, wondering where we'd stop for supper on the way home, and hoping it wouldn't turn out to be a McDonald's. Half the drive would be down a pretty mountain canyon with some scattered tourist joints, but even at the height of the season, most of them close early.

Mike had been up for close to twenty hours by then. He'd worked an eight-hour night shift the night before, then rowed and fished all day in the wind. We had a three-hour drive ahead of us, but he didn't seem tired, although he has a talent for dropping off to sleep suddenly, as if he'd been poleaxed. The conversation will lag for a minute or two, and then the snoring begins. I never feel sorry for him; I just envy his stamina.

We were just about smack in the middle of the lake when the wind died and the water glassed off to reflect the snowfields behind us lit up pink in the last of the sunlight and the rose and charcoal clouds behind them.

And then hundreds of grayling started to rise. Maybe thousands. It's a big lake, and from where we sat it looked like there was a spreading ring on every square foot of it. They were little fish, mostly—when they jumped out of the water they looked coal black against the reflection—but there were some big ones scattered around, too, and we tried to pick out the larger boils and cast to them.

We stayed pretty busy until the light went out and the rises sput-tered down to the odd dimple here and there. But looking back on it, hundreds of rising grayling silhouetted against a mountain sunset must have been one of the most beautiful things I've ever seen. As it is, the memory is only peripheral, and now I think I should have stopped casting long enough to take it in. It's been said that to get to the place where it's no longer about how many fish you catch, you first have to pass through the place where that's exactly what it *is* about. Apparently, it's a long journey.

Then it was dark and the wind came up again, real cold this time, and of course it was blowing right off the corner of the lake we were headed for. I was on the oars by then, and as I was rowing on up the lake I got a mosquito bite on the back of my hand. I had to wonder how a mosquito could get to the middle of a big lake in a cold wind strong enough to make a grown man strain at a pair of seven-foot oars. Determination, I guess.

CHAPTER 13

If grayling are considered a second-class fish, then carp must be somewhere off the bottom of the list, in the same footnote with bowfins and suckers. Or at least they used to be.

It's actually interesting what's happened with carp in the last ten years or so. It wasn't that long ago that if you fished for carp at all you were considered to be some kind of a smart-ass, and if you fished for them with a fly rod, it was easy enough to find a purist who would be offended either by you or by the fish. It was never quite clear which.

This was just another side of the elitism that has always been ignored by a large number of fishermen—to their credit—but that has nonetheless always been part of the sport. It's what once allowed dry fly fishers to look down their noses at wet fly fishers, salmon guys to look down on trout guys, and so on.

This active prejudice against carp among some fly fishers is fairly new for the same reason that many states still don't have specific laws against cannibalism: Up until recently, both were unthinkable. But as soon as a few curious fishermen started fooling around with carp on a fly rod, some others felt they had to get huffy about it—

it was almost required—although to be fair, most couldn't have cared less one way or the other. It either sounded interesting or it didn't, and that was the end of it.

In case you haven't noticed, there really are some enormous and enormously fragile egos in fishing. The reasons for that are potentially too sad to get into, but I can tell you that having a big ego is like owning one of those huge dogs that crap on the floor and eat the couch if they don't get constant attention. I mean, it's just fishing, and the best the big non-angling world can say about any of us is that we're harmless.

When I first got into them, I was in that faction that thought of going after carp with a fly rod as a combination practical joke and a not-so-subtle comment on the class wars that have always gone on in fly-fishing. What I mean is, I wanted to do it precisely *because* some people would be offended.

But then I tried it and I couldn't catch them, which surprised the hell out of me. I mean, when it's all said and done, I'm not a bad fisherman, at least in recognizable situations. When I mentioned that to a highbrow I know, he said, "What do you mean you couldn't catch them? They're only carp." Up till then, that's how I'd felt about it, too.

By the time I did learn how to catch them (and it took a while), I'd gotten pretty intrigued. Carp sometimes act more like cattle than like predators, but they'll eat just about anything a trout would eat in the same water: aquatic and terrestrial insects, crustaceans, crawdads, that kind of thing. They say they're not very interested in forage fish, but too many carp have been caught on Woolly Buggers and Muddlers to entirely rule that out. My theory is, carp don't actively chase minnows, but they'll eat a sick or injured one that's easy prey.

In most lakes and ponds, carp spend a lot of time feeding on or near the bottom, but they'll also cruise just under the surface looking for odds and ends, and sometimes you'll see them rising (or "clooping" as the English call it) to anything from grasshoppers to mayfly spinners to cottonwood seeds.

Early on I tried to put together a fly selection specifically for carp, but it started to dissolve when I discovered that the best cottonwood seed imitation was a size 16 or 18 Parachute Royal Wulff. Now I fish for them out of my trout boxes, and some of the specialty carp patterns I tried turned out to be pretty good for trout, too, especially the bottom-crawling nymphs and crawdad sorts of things. I guess a good fly is a good fly, regardless of what eats it.

If you can bring yourself to look at carp objectively, they should rate well as a game fish. They're often highly visible (at least if you have a good eye), but they're also shy and easy to spook: more so when they're cruising near the surface in clear water, less when they have their faces in the mud on the bottom. They can be gullible, but more often they're as particular as a brown trout about what they'll eat. You often have to cast accurately and precisely to get them to strike, and with a very light touch to keep from spooking them. They'll take a fly readily if you do absolutely everything right, but almost everything usually won't get it. They fight long and hard enough that landing one is never a foregone conclusion. And they're big. A five-pound carp is just a nice fish, and much larger ones are caught regularly. To even begin to impress anyone with a carp, you pretty much have to crack ten pounds.

And they're handsome in their own way. A typical common carp is a hard, muscular, robust, well-proportioned fish, overall bronze to gold with large scales that form a kind of dark herringbone pattern, with orange highlights on the face, fins, and tail. The mouth is turned down, round, and toothless. Viewed straight on, it looks like the bell of a clarinet made of wet leather.

Overall, they manage to come off as dignified. Next to a big, healthy ten-pound carp, a twelve-inch brook trout can look like a minnow in a clown suit.

And they're supposed to be a good food fish, to the point that in some cultures they're considered to be a delicacy. The trick, they say, is to get smaller fish from cool, clear water. (The carp in some of the mountain reservoirs here in Colorado would do.) I've never eaten a carp and probably never will, but if I ever decided to, I know I could do it without an ounce of guilt, whereas eating a wild trout these days can turn into a moral chess game that you will inevitably lose.

In fact, there are some regional cuisines based on carp that most of us have never tried or even heard of. Mike Clark used to catch carp by accident while fishing for big rainbows in a cold, clear reservoir in Wyoming. He'd keep them and give them to a woman he knew who was from "somewhere in Europe." She thought they were delicious and was happy to get them, but she wanted them uncleaned because she used the innards in one of her recipes.

"What did she do with the guts?" I asked him once.

He said, "I didn't ask. Didn't want to know."

Most of the game fish we go after with a fly rod *are* considered to be good to eat—whether we end up eating them or not—because that's what the sport was once about, but it's not actually a requirement. A lot of fishermen go nuts over tarpon, but I'm told they're inedible or, to be completely accurate, edible only in the sense that they're not poisonous. When I was in Florida a few years ago, a man told me they once tried to make cat food out of tarpon, but the cats wouldn't eat it and the tarpon were saved.

For some reason, America is one of the few places on earth where carp aren't very well thought of. Almost everywhere else they're found, from Europe to Asia, they're highly respected as a food and game fish. Common carp were introduced into North America in the late 1800s for food and sport, and in terms of their numbers and their range, they're much more successful than our two other famous imports, the ring-necked pheasant and the brown trout. But for complicated reasons, they just never quite caught on here, and most of us grew up thinking of them as a trash fish if we thought of them at all.

But more and more fly fishers are getting interested in carp these days, in the same way they started to get turned on to large-mouth bass in the 1970s. You don't have to apologize for being a bass fisherman anymore, but you're still supposed to be sheepish about fishing for carp, or "the lowly carp," as one fishing writer recently said. You don't hear too many outright apologies, but some fly fishers refer to carp euphemistically, calling them backyard bonefish or Rocky Mountain gefilte fish (not to be confused with Coney Island whitefish) and claim to go after them only when nothing else is biting.

I do usually fish for them when nothing else is biting, but that's just because carp will be feeding happily on days so bright that bass are sulking on the bottom and so hot that trout are gasping at spring holes just to stay alive. Where some game fish seem prissy and spoiled, carp work dawn to dusk. If you wanted a fish that could sip white wine and discuss Italian poetry, you'd look for a trout. If you needed a ditch dug, you'd hire a carp.

There are signs that carp are gradually creeping toward respectability, even among some of those fishermen who feel it's up to them to decide what's respectable and what's not. And things do change. You can now pay thousands of dollars a day to fish for Atlantic salmon, but up and down the East Coast they were once pitchforked out of rivers and plowed into fields as fertilizer by settlers from Europe who thought carp tasted good.

Carp probably owe some of their budding reputation to saltwater fly-fishing because the comparison with bonefish is inescapable. Carp are often found tailing and mudding in shallow water just like bonefish—they're both bottom feeders—and they even look alike in some ways. They're both streamlined, plain but impressive, with the sloping foreheads and sad eyes of fish that spend their lives looking down, and mouths set low on their faces. Thinking of either fish as beautiful is an acquired taste. No less an expert than Al McClane once described bonefish as having a small mouth under a "piglike snout."

Fly-fishing for carp and bonefish is similar enough that if you can catch one, you've got a decent start on the other. A friend of mine from Texas even fishes his bonefish flies for carp and does well. He says the main differences between the two fish are that carp get bigger and there are more of them.

But luckily most fly fishers still don't want to fish for carp, so at least for now the fish haven't lost their Bohemian charm, and those of us who do fish for them now and then can still be happy misfits. I mean, try to imagine that you're one of the first few people who discovered that trout were sort of fun to catch on flies, but no one else was on to it yet, so you had river after river full of the things pretty much to yourself.

I can make a good case for carp. There *is* more interest than there used to be, and a friend recently told me (apparently without irony) that he thought they were "the fish of the future." But I don't know if carp will ever really come into their own or not. (And if they do, what the hell will *that* mean?) The way fly-fishing is now, I have trouble picturing it: A selection of expensive carp rods from a major rod maker? Guides poling carp boats around farm ponds for $450 a day? I guess it's possible.

Of course, there is a book now, *Carp on the Fly,* by Barry Reynolds, Brad Befus, John Berryman, and Dave Whitlock, and at least one organization, the Carp Anglers Group out of Goveland, Illinois. (Thank God they didn't call it Carp Unlimited.) They publish a bimonthly newsletter, they want to set up local chapters, and one of their goals is to "gain acceptance of the carp as an exciting and challenging game fish." But why?

I'm sure these are good-hearted, well-meaning folks, but it might be best if they kept this under their hats. So far, American carp fisheries are an unspoiled, mostly undiscovered resource— even if some of them aren't especially scenic—and the last thing they need is promotion. I also hope this doesn't blow up in their faces. That is, I hope that twenty years from now the founding fathers of the Carp Anglers Group aren't sitting around complaining about how all the good carp ditches are just too damned crowded these days.

Stranger things have happened, and the earliest signs may already be visible. For instance, my friend Chris Schrantz has what amounts to a carp lease. It's a beautiful, quiet, thirty- or forty-acre pond, ringed in cattails, melodious with bullfrogs and yellow-headed blackbirds, and with a magnificent view of the snowcapped

Front Range to the west. The owner asked Chris, who's a fishing guide, to check out the pond to see if maybe they could work out a deal on the fishing. When Chris reported back that the thing was full of big carp, the guy said, "Okay, never mind," and Chris said, "Well, now wait a minute . . ."

The average size is probably around eight or ten pounds, but carp over twenty pounds have come out of there on flies, and larger ones have been hooked but not landed. The way things are, it came dirt cheap. If this same lake were full of largemouth bass or trout even a third the size of the carp that live there, a lease would be way out of the price range of everyone I know.

I've fished this lake twice now, both times with Chris and Vince. Since Vince is a casting instructor, I want to think he's interested in carp mostly because of the long-distance, pinpoint accuracy of the casts it takes to catch them, but then he has the enthusiasm of a big puppy, so maybe he just likes them because they're fish.

The same seems true of Chris. As an on-duty guide or just a fisherman, he's caught all manner of impressive game fish (sea-run brown trout in Argentina, steelhead, you name it), but judging from how well and carefully he fishes for them, carp seem as good as anything else.

Of course, I'm just guessing because none of us has ever talked much about the why of it. It's just that most of the people I know who fly-fish are the same ones who caught tadpoles in peanut butter jars as kids and got yelled at by their mothers because they came home late and all muddy. We spend more money and use better tackle now, but aside from that, not much has changed: Here's a neat-looking wild critter of some kind, and you somehow got your hands on it against the odds. You admire it, try not to let it bite you, and then let it go. It almost doesn't matter what it is.

We had one great morning last summer on Chris's lease. It was a hot, bright, windless day without so much as a ripple on the water, and the fish were cruising just under the surface, feeding on something (who knows what?) about three or four inches deep. Sometimes they were in twos and threes, sometimes in loose pods of as many as a dozen. The water was murky—as carp water tends to be—and the fish would materialize and then fade away like ghosts, so that half the time you weren't quite sure where they were or which one was the lead fish. Sometimes—often, in fact—they were there and gone so quickly you didn't have time for a cast.

The keys to this kind of carp fishing are casting accuracy, the sink rate of your fly, and its size, pretty much in that order. Cruising carp will sometimes move for a fly, but it's best if they swim right up on it, especially in dark water. You want to put the fly down gently as close to the fish as possible without spooking him. Depending on his speed and the clarity of the water, that can be anywhere from six inches to six feet. The fly should then sink down to his level so that when he gets to it, it's right in front of his nose, where you may or may not want to give it a little twitch or a slow pull. With any luck, he'll inhale it without so much as having to turn his head.

The take can be so slow and gentle that you can't see it, and you won't feel it if you're not stripping the fly. Sometimes a fish will speed up a little and then stop for a second when he eats the fly. Other times you can see the floating part of your leader bump forward or straighten out, but you can't count on either of those things. Setting the hook becomes an educated guess: something you eventually learn how to do without ever quite knowing how you do it.

In spots like this I usually tie on a nondescript nymph, such as a Hare's Ear, in a size 12 or 14. On days when the fish seem unusually shy, I'll fish a size 16 on a dead sink. If they're hungry and aggressive, I'll try a size 8 or 10 and strip it to make it seem alive. But those are just rules of thumb. Most days you have to feel out the fish by trying this and that, looking for just the right combination of cast and sink, pattern and retrieve.

You have to hunt up visible fish—blind casting is pretty much useless—and opportunities for miscalculations and screwups are endless. There are times when the fish spook at a cast that couldn't have been better, at the mere presence of the boat, the dipping of an oar, a footfall on the deck, a raised fly rod, or something completely out of your control, like the shadow of a passing osprey. Even when it all goes right, you can miss the strike and blow up a pod of a dozen ten-pounders. When that happens—a hundred and twenty pounds of fish gone forever in a huge, brown boil—you feel desolate and helpless, even though they're only carp.

The thing is, while you're trying to catch them at least, they're fish and you're a fisherman, and that's the end of it. I used to like fishing because I thought it had some larger significance. Now I like fishing because it's the one thing I can think of that probably doesn't. It's interesting how little difference that makes.

Between seven-thirty and eleven in the morning that day, Chris, Vince, and I landed seven or eight fish among the three of us, all fishing lightly weighted nymphs in about a size 10 or 12. The smallest was six pounds and the largest was one Chris got that I guessed at twelve pounds, more or less, although now that I look at the photos, I think it must have been more like fifteen.

Of course, it's hard to tell from a snapshot. Chris is small and wiry, and when he holds a big fish he can make it look bigger. Vince is tall and broad-shouldered, so if he were holding the same fish it would look smaller.

Chris landed that big carp in under five minutes on a 5-weight graphite rod—an impressive performance. I took more time to land some smaller fish, but I was using a bamboo rod: a 1960s vintage, 7-weight Orvis Battenkill. I almost always use split bamboo fly rods for carp. That's mostly because I just like the rods, but if someone wants to be offended, I can't say that would bother me.

Chapter 14

I f it were my job to name this little stream just over the Colorado line in southern Wyoming, I'd call it Birch Creek because the mile or so of it that Vince and I fished is lined with dense water birch. Choked with it, actually. In his book *Trees of North America,* C. Frank Brockman describes the water birch as a small, shrubby tree that "commonly forms impenetrable thickets, especially along streams." "Impenetrable" sounds final, but it takes on one more dimension when you're trying to cast a 7½-foot fly rod.

This stream flows down a steep little canyon that's thickly wooded to the ridge tops in tall, straight fir and lodgepole pine. The forest effectively narrows the already thin gulch and raises its lip by another forty or fifty feet on each side. A birch seedling that takes hold along the creek has to grow almost horizontally just above the high-water line until it reaches the narrow ribbon of sunlight that lets it turn upward. The mature trees are now twenty feet tall and roughly *L*-shaped, with multiple trunks ten inches around. In some places, the foliage from either bank meets in the middle of the stream, casting stripes of perpetual shade on the water.

There's a good flow here in the summer and the stream is fast and loud, but there are smooth slicks, pockets, and some deep, green, shady pools that hold fat brown trout to ten or twelve inches, plus a few smaller brook trout. Or at least that's what we caught in one stretch of it on one day. What it actually holds could be a secret that two fishermen just passing through aren't likely to learn.

Fly-casting on this stream is difficult in most spots and impossible in others. Those of us who spend a lot of time on small brushy creeks have learned to use roll casts, sidearm casts, steeple casts, dapping casts, bow and arrow casts (with mixed results for me), and a sort of nail-driving, half-aerial roll cast that, as far as I know, has never been named. Still, there were spots where we just couldn't put a fly—however badly we wanted to—and moving to a better angle was either entirely out of the question or at least more trouble than it was worth.

Making headway up the creek isn't much easier than casting. In some places it seems like you just can't go any farther, either in the water or through the thickets on the banks, although eventually you somehow splash or crash through to the next pool, now and then saving yourself by using a water birch limb as a handle.

The stream is out of the way—almost but not quite hidden—and there are bigger, better streams in the area with much easier access, so I don't think many people bother to fish it. It can't be unknown, but one look into that tangle of birch and pocket water and you know you'll be exhausted and frustrated within fifty yards. I know a lot of fishermen who'd say that if they were going to work that hard, they'd want bigger trout. Anyway, there's no fisherman's trail (not even near the road), no boot prints in the occasional patches of mud, and the trout are happy and eager.

I guess Vince and I also had to be sort of happy and eager to fish it, but there was something meaningful about the way we'd stumbled on the place.

We'd been camped farther down the valley, and we were taking day hikes into the upper reaches of the Encampment River to fish and explore. Things were going well enough, but the first night we realized that we'd unknowingly set up camp near a mob of dirt bikers. I don't like dirt bikes because of their noise, dust, and stink—three of the countless things I go into the woods to get away from. But these guys seemed to be riding legally on the dirt roads, and since I'd ridden in to those good trout lakes earlier that season on the back of an all-terrain vehicle, I just couldn't manage the complicated logic by which it would be okay for me but not for them. Vince and I shrugged at each other and went fishing. Multiple use, live and let live.

When we hiked into the Encampment Wilderness the next day, we stopped to check the trailhead registration box. This is where you're supposed to fill out a form saying who you are, how many there are in your party, what the date is, how long you plan to stay, and the "purpose of your visit," which could well be fishing. I like to look these things over to get an idea how much fishing pressure there's been in the last few weeks. I've been told by Forest Service workers that only about a quarter of the people actually fill out the forms, so I do what they do: count the fishermen and multiply by four.

I opened the box and on top of the stack of forms was a handwritten note saying, in great big letters, "WYOMING ONLY—NO GREENIES!" In case you don't know, Greenies are Colorado fishermen (with green license plates on our pickups) who pay seventy dollars for a nonresident season fishing license. The state of Wyoming seems more than happy to take the money, but some citizens would just as soon not have out-of-staters catching their trout. I can't say I entirely blame them.

The note wasn't really threatening—just someone getting it off his chest—but it wasn't what you'd call gracious, either. On the other hand, I calculated that there had been only about a dozen fishermen in there in the last few weeks. You like to think that when you go to some trouble—driving, camping, and hiking—that you'll leave a large chunk of the crowd behind. It's nice when it actually happens.

• • •

That evening back in camp, the bikers were tearing up the place, riding in and through a little brook trout stream, smashing willows, breaking down banks, and whooping and laughing like drunken hyenas. Even when they got far enough away that the noise of the motors almost blended with the breeze in the pines and the laughter died out entirely, we could still see headlights bouncing and skidding in the creek bottom. Unless things are terribly different in Wyoming, that's illegal as hell, not to mention just plain stupid. There also seemed to be more of them than there'd been yesterday, but it was hard to tell for sure in the dark.

Vince and I talked about going down there and yelling at them, but we both know that confrontations like that can turn ugly, especially when you're outnumbered. You wade in convinced that you're right, only to find that right and wrong have nothing to do with what happens next.

We also both know from bitter experience that making the four- to six-hour round-trip drive to the nearest outpost to make a formal complaint would be a pitiful waste of time. Some poor overworked Forest Service ranger would say he'd look into it, but he wouldn't (lack of time, money, and personnel). It wouldn't be his fault, but we'd be mad at him anyway, and we'd have lost a day of fishing. If we saw a Forest Service truck, we'd flag it down, but that would be about the best we could do.

We dredged some luscious venison chops in olive oil and grilled them over pine coals for supper. They would have been wonderful even if we hadn't been as tired and hungry as we were, and I was glad I'd thrown them in the cooler at the last minute before leaving home. That night we turned in early and slept with earplugs.

The next morning we broke camp at dawn and drove on up the valley looking for new digs. At first we entertained the possibility that things were just generally going to hell, but then we decided it was an isolated incident and that anger takes you nowhere. It was probably time to move anyway, and the beauty of a light camp is that it can go anywhere there's enough level ground for tents and a small fire. True, there's a certain shortage of flat spots in and around the Rocky Mountains, but you can always find something, and there always seems to be somewhere else to go.

We crossed Birch Creek where it flowed under a back road through a culvert and stopped to look at it simply because fishermen must look at trout streams. It's in the contract.

Under the tangled canopy of birch the water was clear as air with some pools that looked like they had some depth. Almost within sight of it was a good place to camp with flat spots for the pup tents and standing dead firewood. The stream looked interesting in a neglected sort of way, and we didn't have any particular destination beyond "somewhere else," so we stopped.

It didn't look good at first. We struggled up the creek casting dry flies to what should have been the right places, but we couldn't buy a strike. I don't know what Vince had been fishing, but I'd gone through all five flies that usually work well for me in this kind of water: a Hare's Ear Parachute, an Elk Hair Caddis, a Royal Wulff, and a Dave's Hopper with a Hare's Ear Soft Hackle behind it on a dropper. At one point we looked at each other from a distance of twenty yards through a screen of birch leaves and shrugged.

But as the morning warmed up, we started to see a few bugs—the odd caddis and mayfly—and then Vince hooked a fat, foot-long brown that jumped a foot out of the water. He said, "Hey!" and I crashed down to the stream to look at it as if I'd never seen a trout before.

By late afternoon we were sweaty and exhausted from wading and hiking, and the loud rushing of the stream had washed the noise of motors out of our heads. We'd sniffed arnica, paintbrush, and an unfamiliar wildflower that resembled a snapdragon; examined dipper nests on midstream rocks that looked like little brown igloos made of dead moss; looked at mushrooms (none of which were edible); seen a hermit thrush, Canada jays, and chickadees; lost several flies to the water birch; and caught lots of chubby brown trout. I can't speak for Vince, but for me the edge of paranoia and the urge to pick a fight were gone. This may have been the first time in my life that I'd knowingly used fishing as a sedative, and it had worked.

We took a break on a big rock overlooking a pool. It was a good vantage point, and we spent a few minutes trying to spot trout in the water but couldn't. Then it became obvious that by looming up fifteen feet above the creek with the sun at our backs, we had spooked the fish and they were all hiding under rocks. They may have been pushovers for artificial flies, but shadows from overhead were something they understood.

So we drank the last of our water and looked at a topo map. The creek went on for miles upstream, farther than we could get in a day of hard hiking, let alone at a slow fishing pace. Past that it went off our map and onto the next quadrangle, which we didn't have. It was roadless and steep except for what looked like a half-mile meadow stretch where the contour lines spread out and the blue line of the stream meandered. In this country that could mean long, deep bend pools like a spring creek or a stony riffle with no fish. You'd have to hike up there and see for yourself.

We wouldn't do that. In fact, the plan was to break camp again in the morning and move on. The way things work out, chances are we'll never go back, and if we do we'll probably try one of the half dozen other feeder creeks in those headwaters.

That night's camp was quiet: just the snapping of the fire and a little wind. We were close enough to the dirt road that if a car had passed we'd have heard it or seen its headlights, but none did. And there'd been all the firewood we needed within sight of camp—another sign of little use. I cooked supper and there was that one unpleasant episode where Vince flatly refused to eat his spinach, but otherwise it was what we'd been looking for when we moved camp, and it hadn't been hard to find.

So here was another little trout stream that we'd never heard of, surrounded by another fifty square miles of mostly roadless mountains, forests, and several more streams at least the size of Birch Creek. We were staying in what looked like an old elk hunters' camp, with an improvised cross beam to hang the quarters, but although it was the height of fishing season in a part of the world where the sport is taken very seriously, there were no other fisher-men around.

There *would* be elk in here, also mule deer, black bears, maybe the occasional moose, blue grouse, cottontails, and snowshoe hares, and of course two kinds of trout—maybe three if there are some cutthroats holding out way up high—all scattered around in more open public land than you could adequately explore in ten years.

Somewhere there's a guy who's done it: come to know Birch Creek and the country around it like the back of his hand, found and caught the few sixteen-inch browns that probably live in it somewhere, and either eaten them or released them, depending on how he feels about that.

Maybe he explored a lot of this as a younger man and has now been places in these mountains that he will never see again. That's something you do come to at some point. It's not necessarily a heartbreaker, but it's definitely a milestone. And as quiet as this place still is, maybe it's more crowded now than it used to be. Most places are.

Maybe he's the guy who left the "NO GREENIES" note down in the wilderness area. If so, I can't help thinking I know how he feels. The world changes—gradually or suddenly—and over time the list of things you can take for granted gets shorter and shorter. That has to be *somebody's* fault, right?

As I said, I no longer think there's an unlimited supply of vacant land and overlooked streams, but at the same time I've always been able to find just that when I needed it, provided I was willing to put in the time and effort.

Sometimes that effort is a long, steep hike. Other times it's just a quiet drive on back roads. There are days when the struggle pays off or when you just need struggle for its own sake, and there are days when it's almost too easy. The biggest cutthroat I landed south of Canada that year was within sight of Mike Price's Suburban. The fish was rising quietly at the lip of a culvert under a county road in the Bighorn Mountains, so close to the gravel turnout that I could hear the tick of the engine cooling. Of course, it helped that Mike had fished the stream before and not only knew where that trout lived but also that he'd bite a size 16 Royal Wulff.

Over the years I've fully explored a handful of these little mountain creeks, casually fished a few dozen others, and have hiked or driven past dozens or maybe even hundreds more on the way to somewhere else—and I've barely scratched the surface. There are thousands of them in the American West and that many more over the border in Alberta and British Columbia. Some days it worries me that I'll never be able to get to all of them.

CHAPTER 15

That kind of thing seems common among fishermen: When we're not worrying that there's too little good water left, we worry that there's too much and life is short. It makes a few of us frantic, a few greedy, and a few others sad, but for most it just works out to a kind of low-grade wanderlust.

There are lots of places you have to fish simply because you've never fished there—and the more you can leave it at that, the happier you'll be. But when you travel to fish, it's still worth asking yourself what you're after, just to avoid the kind of tail chasing that comes from indecision. There's no right answer: It could be bigger fish, or new fish, or the same old fish eating different flies in strange new surroundings, or strange new surroundings that turn out to be eerily familiar.

Or maybe it has less to do with the fish than you think. Maybe you just want to drive until you're lost on unmarked dirt roads or ride in a float plane and spend foreign money. It's even possible that you just want to be gone, and you're carrying a fly rod to give yourself a vague sense of purpose.

In the years I've been fly-fishing, I've traveled to a few faraway places and it's almost always been worth it however it turned out. There were big bass in Texas, huge brook trout in Labrador, perfect west slope cutthroats in British Columbia, a grilse run in New Brunswick, salmon and rainbows in Alaska, big grayling in the Northwest Territories, and so on, not to mention the new scenery, people, accents, boats, and planes to go with them.

Even the Atlantic salmon trip to Scotland was worthwhile. I mean, how often do you have a chance to get skunked while casting a fourteen-foot spey rod in the shadow of a castle built two hundred years before the American Revolution? A fish or two would have been nice, but you learn early that you can't have everything on every trip.

But since I moved from the Midwest to the Rocky Mountains a little over three decades ago, I've done most of my fishing pretty close to home, say, within a one- or two-day drive, which puts four or five western states, parts of two Canadian provinces, and some of the best trout fishing in North America within range.

I could say it's more efficient that way—more fishing for the time and money spent, and with no travel agents, ironclad itineraries, airline security, or lost luggage—and that would be true enough. But it's just as true to say that I moved west in the late '60s to look around and I'm still looking.

Mostly I'm not trying to find anything in particular, just a lake, stream, or pond I've never fished before. I try to explore out of pure inquisitiveness, but at the same time, the old rules of thumb apply: All things being equal, more fish are better than fewer fish; big fish are better than little ones; wild fish are better than stockers.

Sometimes I'll decide to fish a stream just because it's there—especially if not too many people *know* it's there—but for the most part, I follow tips and rumors. Once, almost all fishing operated on this kind of subculture grapevine. Back then it was possible to keep a secret for as long as several seasons, and even when it leaked out, it leaked slowly, like a tire you could still limp another fifty miles on.

Now news travels with brutal efficiency through a much larger population of fly fishers, so if you know something, it's wise to keep your mouth shut, and if someone kindly lets you in on something, you should consider yourself honor bound not to repeat it without permission. Those two rules have always applied, but they're more important now than they used to be. Just remember, you're not paranoid if they really *are* out to get you.

People look to the Internet for almost everything now, but I think it's best not to depend on it for really choice fishing information. I don't know too much about this monster (I value my time and my privacy too much to be plugged into it), but I understand that Web sites can get thousands of hits per hour and that people regularly copy their e-mails to their five hundred closest friends, who all do the same, and so on ad infinitum. By the time you hear about a secret fishing spot electronically, you have to figure every fisherman in the world knows about it and half of them are already there.

I think the best tips on fishing spots still travel the way they always have: face to face among friends. I get most of my best information from a small circle of friends—Mike Price, Mike Clark, A.K., Ed, Vince, Chris—and I usually pass on what little I find out on my own in the same company. Most of us have lived and fished in the same area for many years and have a few other things in common, too. We're middle-aged (or close to it on one end or the other), somewhat reclusive, and—with the possible exception of Chris, a.k.a. Mister Mellow—we have less patience with people than we do with fish. For the most part, we're all looking for the same thing: quiet places that aren't overrun. Great big fish are nice—and they're out there to be found—but the more we do this, the more affection we end up having for pretty little wild fish.

And we've come to trust each other. That is, if one of the guys tells me about a beaver pond with some sixteen-inch brookies in it, I know he's not hallucinating over a couple of ten-inchers. (If I go there and don't see the big fish, I don't assume they were never there; I assume I was too clumsy and spooked them.) I also know that if I spill the beans about some sweet little something I've found, it won't go any further.

I don't mean to say that any of these guys is perfect. I never looked for perfect people to be my friends for fear of going through life friendless. It's just that we get along, see most things the same way, and can disagree peacefully. Some of us can talk politics for hours and get mad as hell, though not at each other, but with others it's a lot easier to travel and fish together if we *don't* talk politics, except maybe in the most general terms. I mean, the fate of democracy is one thing, but someone you can fish with is another.

Having good, trusted friends who get along and fish well probably isn't something you can coldly list as a fishing tactic. I just had to mention it because although I think of myself as a self-sufficient and cagey fisherman, in one way or another I owe most of the best fishing I've had to my friends.

But then I *will* say that I've come up with a few good spots on my own, almost all of which I've shared with the boys. Prospecting for places to fish that everyone and his brother doesn't already know about doesn't take anything except curiosity and time, but when it's done well it's an art form.

Over the years I've had some luck getting permission to fish farm ponds and stretches of creek running through ranches. Granted, that's a lot harder than it used to be, and in some places it's gotten to be well nigh impossible. Neighborliness is the first thing that suffers when an area starts to get crowded; people are more suspicious of strangers than they used to be; and many of them are now worried—with good reason—that if you slip on a cow turd on their property, you'll sue them to the tune of twenty million dollars for emotional damage.

It's also true that if the fishing is any good at all for something besides carp, the landowner now probably understands that rather than letting the odd polite stranger fish it for free or for a few dollars, he can lease it to a club for enough money to help with the taxes.

I've run into all those things and more in recent years, and it does get discouraging at times. Still, if you've had your eye on a pretty little piece of water somewhere, it can't hurt to ask. All the guy can say is no.

As far as I can tell, the rules here haven't changed since I was a kid in the Midwest: You go to the front door like a gentleman, tip your hat, and state your business briefly and politely. If you live just up the road and could pass for a neighbor, go ahead and say that (it still counts in some places) and you could mention that you'd certainly be willing to pay a small trespass fee, but don't pitch the guy. People are on to salesmanship, and they have no tolerance for it.

If the answer is no, say thanks anyway, sorry to bother you, and leave. Don't argue. It's rude and it's pointless.

I don't actually have the demographics to prove it, but I think this works better in areas far from cities and new developments, and in places where fishing isn't the big tourist industry. It seems like most rural landowners feel the same way I do about fishermen: A few of them are fine, but too many amount to a plague.

I tend to do this sort of thing casually and in person, but I've known fishermen who were bulldogs about it. They'd do things like go down to the courthouse to study county maps and aerial photos, and then look up the ownership records on hidden ponds, rural reservoirs, and obscure stretches of small streams. I've never gone to that kind of trouble myself, but I've looked over their shoulders a few times and it's been pretty educational. If nothing else, I've always been amazed that even in areas where I've fished for years, there's a hell of a lot more water than I thought.

But my favorite place to prospect for fishing spots is on public land, and through my usual combination of skill and dumb luck, I happen to live where there's a lot of it. National parks, national forests, wilderness areas, state forests, state and federal wildlife areas, Bureau of Land Management properties, you name it.

Virtually all of the most popular and heavily fished rivers and lakes are on public land, but so are many more remote or at least out-of-the-way mountain lakes, strings of beaver ponds, and hundreds of miles of stream that don't get much attention.

Tributaries to good trout streams are always a fair bet, and so are the headwaters of tailwater rivers. Tailwater fisheries are like vacuums: They suck up every fisherman that comes near them, often leaving hundreds of miles of headwater creeks all but vacant.

I like to pick trail-less areas or creeks that I've never heard any-thing about. I'll look at a big map—say, one that covers an entire national forest—and then check topographic maps for more detail. Eventually, something stands out: a mile of stream flowing through a gorge, while the trail loops around onto easier terrain; a chain of beaver ponds far up a creek that's known to have trout in it but that everyone says is nothing special.

You do run up against dead ends. Maybe that trail loops around the gorge because the gorge is impassable, with sheer cliffs and water too fast and deep to wade. You know there are trout in there because there are trout above and below it, and they're probably undisturbed and as big as they can get.

It's impossible to get in there, but you had to go look. Then again, maybe in September or October when the water is down, you could just squeeze through. So—maybe this fall, maybe next—you hike back in there, only to find that the water is still too deep and, as you might expect, the cliffs are still too steep. At first you might be a little pissed—you walked miles, killed a whole day—but then the little canyon is still beautiful and, come to think of it, there's nothing wrong with having a few trout in the world that may never see a hook.

Honestly, most of these little adventures turn out to be successful only because I satisfied my curiosity and had a nice hike in the mountains. With that in mind, I try to explore on days when catch-ing a fish would be nice, but getting blanked on some pretty new water would be okay, too. But I've also found a few real gems that I'd never have known about if I hadn't bothered to go look.

There was the stretch of feeder creek miles back into a national park (and a half mile off the nearest trail) that had exactly five good pools, and each one gave up exactly one fat brook trout in spawn-ing colors. There wasn't a lot of good water to fish, but it had been a long, hard hike, and after five trout it was time to start back any-way.

There's also the wilderness area creek above a waterfall (and, again, off the trail) where I've caught more than one big cutthroat in water you'd think wouldn't hold much more than five-inchers.

Even if I don't find something I'll ever want to go back to, I still know something I didn't know before, so when someone points at a map and asks, "You ever fish up in here?" I can say, "Yup, full of little brookies, but it's real pretty and you probably won't see anyone."

The assumption is that you're always looking for something fabulous, not in some poetically left-handed sense, but the real nuts-and-bolts stuff of fishing: the secret spot with the huge trout. Maybe you are at first, but eventually it just comes down to knowing something you didn't know before. It's not that you don't find the great spots now and then—you do if you keep at it. It's just that you're no longer disappointed when you don't find them, and when you do, it's a complete surprise.

You spill the beans about most of it to your friends, but sometimes you hold on to something for a while, just to savor it, and sometimes you hold on to something forever—just because.

This last summer, Ed arrived at my house after a solitary four-day backpack trip into some remote country on the West Slope. He'd packed a number of miles up a small, rugged drainage, set up a light base camp, and then done day trips even higher up. He'd caught lots of brookies and cutthroats; lived on granola and powdered milk mixed together in a plastic bag (just add filtered creek water); weathered rain every day—sometimes all day; and read himself to sleep at night with either a mystery novel or a book of poems by the T'ang dynasty poet Han-Shan. (Ed isn't the only person I've heard claim to read poetry in camp, but he's among the few who actually do it.)

When Ed arrived at my place, we hosed the mud off his gear and hung it out to dry, did a load of laundry, and got him a decent meal. Then he ran down most of the trip for me, showing me a few places on my big topo map but also carefully leaving out a thing or two without apology.

We've been friends a long time, and although we believe in generosity, we also both think that anyone who goes to that kind of trouble to explore remote water deserves whatever secrets he cares to keep. I couldn't help but wonder, but in fact he'd given me all I needed. If I had the guts to grunt all the way back in there and spend the time, I'd find the places he hadn't told me about, and I'd understand why.

Ed said he was pretty tired, so I knew it would be tough. I've spent a large part of my life outdoors trying to keep up with this guy and helplessly watching his back disappear up a steep trail. I could probably still do it, but it would take me longer, and I may find that I *have* to do it. I get in a lot of fishing myself—as much as I want to most years—and I like to keep a little something to myself now and then, too, but when a friend does something great without me, I can still get a little jealous.

A lot of this stuff takes no less than a full, hard summer day to fish (most of it spent hiking) or even longer if you really want to get serious. But a stream doesn't have to be miles back into a wilderness area to be overlooked.

Most of the obvious and popular public lands come in huge chunks. Colorado's Rocky Mountain National Park—a twenty-minute drive from my house—covers a little over four hundred square miles. (Add the surrounding contiguous chunks of Roosevelt, Arapaho and Routt national forests and it begins to approach two thousand square miles.) When a fisherman looks at a detailed map of the park, all he can see are the blue lines of streams flowing out of the blue dots of lakes to form the headwaters of three rivers. It's a real embarrassment of riches.

But in other places the public land comes in odd notches and corners, sometimes all but blocked off by private posted land. Access to some of these areas is ticklish, but it can be worth sorting out because most people won't go to the trouble.

Like that pretty little trout stream not too far from my new house, the one Rick, Don, and I hiked in to in the spring. At first glance at a good map it seems to be completely barricaded by private land, but there's that back door we found without going to much trouble at all if you don't count the hike in.

For some reason, I haven't gone back there yet. No telling why. Maybe all I needed to do was locate the route in, prove to myself that there are, in fact, some trout in it, and end up knowing something I didn't know before. But of course I will go back there eventually, if only because it's close to home and I now know the way.

There's even a spot not far from here where a single landowner separates the county road from that corner of national forest, and it might be possible to finesse access there. Leon, the horse guy, knows everyone in the valley, so I might be able to wangle an introduction. I've made that sort of thing work before if only because it can be made to sound so reasonable: "Hi, I'm your neighbor from down the road. I don't want to fish on your place, I just want to walk across it to get on the public water upstream." Who could resist that, combined with my boyish smile?

CHAPTER 16

I was supposed to meet A.K. at some warm-water ponds we know of here in the county. It was another one of those bright, motionless, deadly hot western summer days that might or might not be freshened up by an afternoon thunderstorm. In terms of comfort, you have to think hot and wear shorts, the lightest canvas shirt you own, and a straw hat you can soak in pond water and let evaporate on your head. And no, the hat will never look or smell quite the same again.

You also have to slather yourself with the kind of industrial-strength sunscreen that feels like axle grease on your skin, runs into your eyes and stings, collects dust, and just generally makes you feel nasty. I hate the stuff, but I've been a stickler about using it ever since I met an old fisherman years ago who'd lost the tops of his ears and most of his nose to skin cancer. When he caught me staring, he smiled and said, "I used to be better looking."

I was supposed to meet A.K. at two, right at the center of the day's heat, and I wonder now why we weren't meeting on a trout stream up in the nearby foothills, where it would have been cooler. But then this isn't the kind of thing that has to make sense. I'd just fished Birch Creek and some other new water up in Wyoming, so it would have been time to go fish an old standby, if only because you have to keep an eye on your home water. This is one of the reasons why being a fisherman takes a lifetime.

Anyway, it was breathless and well into the nineties when I left home. On the drive out to the ponds, the fields and stands of cottonwoods had that brilliant midday stillness about them—no breeze, no birdsong, cattle asleep on their feet—and I saw a shimmer of mirage glide across the paved road in front of me like a chrome snake.

My gear was pretty spartan. I carried it out to the pickup in a single load, including two big bottles of water. I'd drink one slowly on the drive out, then chug the other before I walked in to the pond. This is a way of lightening the load—by avoiding dehydration without having to lug water.

Another way is to wade wet, in cutoff blue jeans and old tennis shoes, instead of wearing the regulation hip boots. I guess I was beginning to wonder if life was getting a little more complicated than it had to be, and that was making me reexamine some of the things I did automatically, like wearing waders on a hot day. You know, going to some trouble to stay dry when, once you stop and think about it, getting wet would be easier and feel better, too. It may not seem like much, but then simplicity comes in small packages.

I'd started wading wet on some trout streams, too, because I'd seen guides doing it, and they looked more comfortable than I felt in my rubber pants. But like everything else, it's a toss-up. Waders can make you too hot on a summer day, while wet wading can make you too cold as evening comes on, and there's nothing worse than having your body tell you to get the hell out of the water and warm up right when the fish start biting. One of the first things a fisherman learns is that comfort is elusive.

I could also say that standing bare-legged in the same water the fish are swimming in puts me more in touch with their moods and makes me a more intuitive fisherman. I've actually thought that a time or two—you think all kinds of things in the long silences of fishing—but it's probably not all that sublime. It just seems appropriate that you get wet when you wade into the water, like all the other mammals on the planet, and it also seems right to come home good and dirty after a day of fishing, smelling faintly of mud, decomposed vegetation, marsh gas, and goose poop. As much as I love fly-fishing, there are times when it all seems a little too neat and clean.

A.K. and I had a good half day of fishing that afternoon. There are those who'll wait until almost evening on a hot day like that, but this was when A.K. could make it. He and I hadn't fished together much that season—or the previous year either, come to think of it—and it actually had gotten kind of strange. When I called him to see about going out to the ponds, I started dialing, then had to stop and look up his phone number, which I'd had memorized for the last fifteen or twenty years.

So we got to the ponds a little too early in the day, but then we sort of like to do that anyway. There's no one around (the smarter fishermen are waiting out the heat), you get in five or six hours of fishing instead of two or three, and sunfish and bass *do* bite in the middle of a hot day. True, they'll usually bite better toward evening, but it's fun to be there and watch that happen.

It starts gradually: After a few hours of flat heat and slow fishing, the light begins to slant, shadows begin to grow along the west bank, the air cools slightly, maybe some clouds build to the west to take the sun off, maybe there's a breeze. You begin to notice more songbirds, and there are either more bugs in the air or they buzz louder. A few swirls appear on the water as fish begin to feed near the surface; then become more regular and more aggressive, and among the small, quiet rings there are suddenly some more impressive boils.

A.K. has always said that afternoon fishing is better than morning fishing because mornings start good and peter out, while afternoons just get better and better.

It always seems to me that the instant I become cool and comfortable on a hot day is about when the pond turns on and the fish really start to bite, but that could just be my imagination—fishermen have great imaginations. Anyway, there's a moment of anticipation that sometimes pans out, and when you high-grade the best part of the day on the theory that you're too busy to just go out there and wait for it, you miss all the drama.

We hiked to the back end of the farthest pond from the road: a place that's fairly difficult to fish. The walk in takes a while, and it's a slow, hot slog on a day like this. The wading is hard through tangled marsh, and it can be treacherous with sudden, mucky drop-offs and waterlogged snags to trip on. There are drowned cottonwoods and weeds to grab your flies on the water, and thorny Russian olives and head-high cattails to snare them from behind when you're not looking. It's the kind of place where you wade and cast carefully and understand that this whole business of fly-fishing is sort of a controlled accident anyway.

And then there's a spot where some amateur engineer has hauled in a six-foot sheet of fiberglass and laid it on the sloping, muddy bottom. Over the years it's become slippery and camouflaged with slime, so you don't know it's there until you step on it and it shoots you into the deep water like a playground slide. I think whoever put it there thought it would let him wade out a few extra feet on the soft bottom, but it's in an especially good spot, so there are those who think it's a booby trap.

I've tried coming into these snarly channels in a belly boat from the open water side, but it's actually harder thrashing through the weeds, dragging the tube over the shallow spots, losing flippers. A canoe would be perfect, except you'd have to carry the thing for more than a mile. I'd rather just walk and wade.

Once you get back in there, you'll see the tracks of blue heron, bittern, goose, magpie, muskrat, deer, and raccoon in the odd patches of smooth mud, but seldom human footprints. Once I almost stepped on a snapping turtle as big around as a garbage can lid. He hissed loudly and cocked his head back to strike. The hair on my bare legs stood up and I retreated.

Another time I was attacked by a red-winged blackbird. Apparently I'd gotten too close to a nest, because the male started dive bombing me. I turned around to leave, but the bird kept coming. When I took off my hat to wave him away, he pecked me on the bald spot and drew blood. It was funny later, but at the time it hurt like hell.

Those are the kinds of things that can happen anywhere. They do give the place a wilder feel, and I'd love it just for that, but it so happens the fishing is a little better, too. I don't mean it's fabulous—if it were fabulous there'd be a wide trail pounded in there—but most days the fish do seem slightly dumber and maybe even a little bigger simply by virtue of being left alone.

I know some spots like this because I started fishing these ponds about twenty-five years ago, as much for the food as for the sport. I'd go out there straight from work, and on a good spring or summer evening I'd get a meal of crappies, bluegills, or smallish largemouth bass, maybe some wild asparagus in season, and maybe even a decent photo I could sell with one of the fishing stories I'd begun freelancing. These are pretty ponds in a funky, backwatery kind of way, especially in evening light and when you can keep the power lines out of the frame.

In fact, I got my first camera out there. It was hanging from a low branch of a cottonwood tree at the third pond back on the north end, obviously forgotten by someone. I left it where it was and fished till dark, but when I came back the camera was still there.

On the way out I looked for another car parked on the road, and I even had the film developed to look for possible clues to the owner's identity, but those were just the formalities that would let me say I hadn't stolen the thing. Back there on the bank of that pond, with a fly rod and a stringer of bluegills in one hand and a new camera in the other, I know I heard a voice say, "Tonight you will eat fish, and in the morning you will be a photographer."

I waded wet in those days because I couldn't afford hip boots—

much less a camera—and because I was deeply interested in getting closer to the earth, as we'd have said back then. (Or, as a smart-ass relative who didn't care for my long hair and torn jeans once put it, "You mean returning to the soil? Like compost?")

It had been only a few years since I'd briefly tried to live in New York City—as I once thought all writers were supposed to do—but that hadn't worked out too well, and I ended up in Colorado instead, living simply and fishing for supper. I guess I was fairly poor, but I was proud enough to work and, out West at least, cunning enough to forage supper a few nights a week by honorable means. I was no more of a genius then than I am now, but I was smart enough to realize that if I managed this just right, I could have it made.

I was also smart enough to stop writing about life and love for a while and try some stories about fishing. Apparently I didn't know much about the subjects of great literature (or so some editors claimed), but I *could* now and then manage to catch some fish. Some of those stories sold, and they were the first ones I was ever paid for. What with the odd paycheck from writing and free cameras growing on trees, things were beginning to look up.

I'd been fishing those ponds for several years when I met A.K. We worked together in a fly shop for a while and hit it off pretty well. We both had it bad for fly-fishing, both had a taste for bamboo rods we couldn't afford, both came from the Midwest, and were both refugees from other lives.

One of A.K.'s other lives had been as a working musician, so he wasn't surprised at any of the lifestyle stuff going on around him. Saxophone players have seen it all and have done at least some of it themselves. He used to say things like "Hey, whatever," put up with my occasional hangovers, and only scolded me if I showed up late to go fishing.

I think I introduced A.K. to these ponds, and if I remember that wrong, I at least know we've fished them together off and on for a long time. A.K. has always been a little more of a trout purist than I am, so I don't think he gets quite as sentimental about them as I do. But we're both native Midwesterners who haven't always known where our next meal was coming from, so warm-water fisheries have the same kind of blue-collar romance for both of us: the idea that fish are there for the guy who's hungry and skillful enough to catch a few, and if you want to make a sport out of it, that's okay, too.

And I guess we always got a perverse kick out of fly-fishing seriously for bass and bluegills in the heart of Rocky Mountain trout country and eating some of them at a time when a few of our more snooty fellow fly casters were beginning to think of killing a fish as murder. That's one thing that hasn't changed over the last couple of decades: The fishermen with the most unforgiving ethics are still the ones with plenty of money for groceries.

A lot has happened since then, and it's sort of a relief to both A.K. and me not to be quite so hungry anymore, although I think there are days when we miss that a little. I mean, the real desire for something to eat did put a keen edge on the fishing.

Starting to wade wet again reminded me of all that. I didn't do it with much in mind besides going light and staying cool, but it was good to see that you can naturally come back around to a kind of simplicity again after several decades: back to just a rod and reel, a single fly box, and an old pair of tennis shoes. Never mind that this is easier with some kinds of fishing than with others and that, in the years in between, A.K. and I had spent what to us were small fortunes on tackle. If nothing else, that's been a great comfort to our friends in the fishing business.

I'll also admit that the first few times I waded wet again I had to overcome a vague squeamishness I don't remember from the old days. When you slog bare-legged into a warm-water marsh, with all its unidentified bubbling, gurgling, and plopping, maybe feel something (God knows what) brush your skin, there's something in the human condition that makes you wonder, Is there anything in here that's gonna bite me?

• • •

As I said, we had a pretty good afternoon. At first the fish were a little sluggish and we had to coax them with sunken flies in bright sunlight. I used a brace of nymphs: a good-sized brown damselfly nymph that a bass might like, with a smaller soft hackle behind it on a dropper for bluegills. I fished them deep and slow because that's how I figured the fish would be: deep and slow. Fishing like this can be like searching for the light switch in a strange, dark hotel room: It can take a while, but there's a real sense of victory when you connect.

At one point A.K. got three nice pan-sized bass right in a row fishing a water boatman beetle pattern off a weed bed. Bass are supposed to go for bigger, more specialized flies, but then A.K. has always been the kind of natural fisherman who can bring trout flies to a bass pond and catch fish anyway.

Later on, some big puffy cumulus clouds boiled up and a light breeze came and went, putting a ripply chop on the water. I switched to a chartreuse cork popper and started getting some good bluegills and pumpkinseeds at the surface. I don't know what A.K. was using, but it seemed like every other time I glanced over at him, he was playing a fish. Sometimes I could hear him laughing, and now and then he'd whoop and hold up a good-sized bass or a fat bluegill.

Once he held up a big sunfish and yelled, "Look at these colors!"

With the sun behind him and twenty or thirty yards between us, I could see only the silhouette of the fish, but I hollered back, "That's beautiful, man!" because I knew it was.

On the way out, we stopped on the first patch of solid ground so A.K. could dump some water out of his left hip boot and wring out his sock. I explained that one advantage to wading wet is you can't go in over your waders. He nodded sagely at that. Over the years, inescapable logic has been a benchmark of our friendship.

On the long walk back to the truck, with the fishing over now, we talked about some other things. It turned out A.K.'s life had also gotten a little more complicated lately—which is why we hadn't been fishing together as much as we used to—and, like me, he'd been taking steps to fix that.

To a fisherman, the reality of complications is that they cut into the fishing time, never mind the particulars. We do all have lives away from fishing—like it or not—and sometimes they demand our full attention. At the same time, I can't help thinking that people like us were meant to live simpler lives than we sometimes do, and there are times when I have to wonder what the hell happened. When you're kept off the water, even for just a day, it seems as though the world has gotten off-kilter. You want to agree with Herbert Hoover, who once said, "Going fishing is the only excuse even a cynic will accept." It's not true, but it sure is a pretty thought.

Earlier that summer, I ran into an old poet friend I hadn't seen in over a year. I said, "How are you, Jack?" and he said, "Busy. Busyness is endemic now, you know."

I thought, If a seventy-year-old poet is too busy, what hope is there for me?

People definitely are busy now, at least the way they tell it. Ask people how they are and they're likely to say "Busy" just as predictably as they'd have said "fine" or "can't complain" ten or fifteen years ago.

Some people are busy doing truly heroic tasks, like clothing, educating, and feeding a couple of kids, but the most puzzling are those who don't exactly know why they're busy. Ask them, "Busy doing what?" and they'll say, "I don't know, stuff. There's always something."

It's become an epidemic. People drive angrily, even through this pretty foothills country, because they're too busy to slow down and enjoy the ride. They eat the worst kind of food because they're too busy to even think about eating well, let alone take the time to do it. Even recreation has gotten loud, frantic, and competitive because no one has what you could honestly call free time anymore. Fun has become a desperate business where you have to enjoy yourself in a few precious hours or die trying.

Fishing isn't the worst of it by a long shot, but the pace has quickened there, too, and success seems more important. You'll sometimes even hear fishermen who've just returned from some beautiful and faraway place say it was pretty much a "waste of time" because the body count wasn't high enough.

I've watched my own busyness grow over the years, and a lot of it is just a by-product of becoming a grownup. When I first started fishing those ponds, I wasn't busy worrying about paying my taxes or my health insurance or my mortgage because I didn't make enough money to pay taxes, and I didn't have insurance or a house. I could go back to that in a heartbeat if I wanted to—and it could happen anyway, whether I want it to or not—but for the time being, I guess I'm willing enough to shoulder the load and forge ahead, even if I have to do it skeptically.

But it seems to me that what has us so busy now isn't the big, important stuff, but the small, inconsequential stuff that adds up imperceptibly until it seems like someone has turned up the speed on the treadmill.

There are the forms you have to fill out for almost everything now; the people you pay to do a job who don't do it; the labor-saving devices that don't save any labor; billing errors that can't be fixed; clerks who can't make change; recorded telephone messages that offer you nine different choices, none of which is the one you want, and so on. If you're not careful, you can stay busy for an extra hour a day, seven hours a week, 364 hours a year. That's over two weeks: enough time for two good fishing trips. No single thing stands out for long, but when someone asks you, "Busy doing what?" you say, "Damned if I know, it's just always something."

The scariest part is, I'm the least busy person I know. That is, I make a living writing about fishing, so I'm often very busy fishing, sometimes for weeks at a time. But that not only doesn't count, it amounts to successfully cheating the system without breaking any laws. In fact, if you explain this in just the right way, it will seem completely reasonable to anyone—even an accountant. But I still sometimes get infected with the national disease of impatience. "I don't have time for this" is a common complaint, but fishermen, of all people, should be able to say, "Actually, I *do* have time for this."

My solution has been to unplug myself to some degree, or, as with things like the Internet, never to plug myself in in the first place. Almost everyone I know complains about the horrendous volume, stupidity, and uselessness of their e-mails. They have 428 of the things in there—clogging up valuable electronic thingama-jigs—and pretty soon they're gonna have to spend a whole day going through all of them in case there's something important. These are some of the same people who tell me I've got to get e-mail because of the ease and convenience of it.

Okay, enough. The thing is, if you're feeling driven, you have to ask yourself, Who's doing the driving? and What's the destination? If you don't like your answers, something could be terribly wrong.

Learn to reject sales pitches of all kinds before you even hear them. Way back in the days of traveling salesmen, my Uncle Leonard told me that if they have to come to you, you don't want whatever it is they're selling. If you wanted it, you'd go to them.

Try to tell the truth at all times, if only because, as A.K. once pointed out, then you're not busy trying to remember what you said. Truth itself may be overrated ("Does this dress make my ass look big?" "Yes, it does."), but in the long run, telling the truth is quicker and easier than lying.

Try to live with the idea that, although life presents you with endless chores, some things will just never get done—at least not by you.

Try to do something good for a living, something you enjoy or that at least seems worthwhile. As the old saying goes, If you have a job you love, you will never work.

Few of us can do more than a small handful of things well and with the proper passion, so don't spread yourself too thin if you can help it. Jalaluddin Rumi said, "A thousand half-loves must be forsaken to take one whole heart home."

All of which is easier said than done.

• • •

Walking back from the pond, A.K. and I agreed that being too busy was just a temporary setback for both of us. What else can you think? Then he told me the best dirty joke I'd heard in a long time, and we covered the last two hundred yards to the truck marveling, for the hundredth time, at the god-awful beauty of sunfish. They're one of the things in the world that are so much prettier than they'd have to be, you have to think it means something.

Back at our trucks we went through the usual ritual. At the end of every day of fishing for as far back as I can remember, A.K. and I have shaken hands and declared success, even when the best that could be said for the whole trip is that neither of us drowned. This time it was easy. We'd landed enough good-sized bass and bluegills that, if we'd kept them, we'd each have had more than enough for a decent meal. I think we both still believe that's all any fisherman deserves.

CHAPTER 17

The Green Drake mayflies are one of those venerable hatches here in the West, the kind that'll make you rearrange a whole fishing season if you think you have a chance at hitting one right. These big flies are said not only to bring the really big trout out from wherever they usually hide, but also to make the cagiest old fish giddy enough to eat something like a size 10 Humpy. These are the trout you hardly ever see, either on the surface or in daylight, and whose very existence you aren't always convinced of, but during a Green Drake hatch you'll find them miraculously feeding on dry flies in the middle of the day.

When I first started fly-fishing and heard these stories from older guys, I thought maybe they weren't completely true. (Even if fishermen aren't outright liars, they're at least enthusiastic story-tellers.) As it turns out, the stories were true just often enough to avoid being complete crap, but they weren't a guarantee either.

On some trophy trout streams I've seen sparse Green Drake hatches that weren't thick enough to bring up the big fish, or even many of the little ones. There'd be a Drake here, another one over there twenty minutes later, and all in all you might see a dozen in an afternoon. Every time you'd spot one you'd think, Okay, this could be it, but if the fish were rising at all they were eating little Pale Morning Duns and you couldn't understand it. You and I would pick out the big juicy ones.

I've also seen decent Green Drake hatches on rivers where there really *weren't* any big trout or, I should say, where a big trout was only ten inches long. Not that there's anything wrong with catching ten-inch trout on dry flies.

That had happened earlier in the season when I was busy for a few weeks rediscovering my home water. I'd wandered down to the creek at a random spot between turnouts on a canyon road and found a steep, rocky chute that—once my memory kicked in—I recalled as not being very good.

But then I saw some big bugs over the water that really looked like Green Drakes. The way the light was, I couldn't see their color, but they had those short, chunky bodies and oversized wings, and they were flying with more apparent effort than most mayflies. I'm always suspicious of fishermen who claim to be able to identify insects in the air right down to species, but when you've fished a distinctive hatch for a long time, the nature of the bug imprints itself subconsciously. Just to be sure, I caught one in my hat. It was a Green Drake.

I didn't have any Green Drake patterns in my small stream box, so I used a Hare's Ear Parachute tied on a long-shanked number 12 hook. It was close enough. It was either a short hatch or I'd come in right in the middle of it, but for the next forty-five minutes or so, that little creek gave up some of its biggest fish—which were none *too* big, but still all you could possibly ask for. That was the first Green Drake hatch I'd ever seen on that stream after somewhere between twenty-five and thirty years of fishing it. I thought, Fifteen minutes from home and right by the side of the road: How could I not have known about this?

But now and then you'll stumble on the kind of thing that got the legend started in the first place: a trout stream that's pretty good on a day-to-day basis anyway, but where the Green Drakes come on thick, and suddenly the fish seem to double in size and numbers. You barely believe it. It's as if an old friend you never suspected of being a musician sat down at a piano one day and played Chopin beautifully, and you could never look at him the same way again.

The first good Green Drake hatch I ever saw was years ago on the Henry's Fork of the Snake in Idaho. A.K., Koke, and I had driven up there specifically to hit the Drakes, along with what looked like half the fly fishers in North America. I'd never seen crowds like that outside of a city, and I'd never seen such big trout eating so many big mayflies. It was glorious, and later A.K. said I walked around for the first few days with my mouth hanging open.

But at first I thought there must be something wrong with the hatch because the fish weren't as easy as they were in most of the stories I'd heard. There were lots of Drakes on the water and lots of big rainbows were up feeding at the surface, but the trout seemed bored by my flies and my drifts. They acted like I'd just launched into the oldest joke in the world, and they'd turn away before I even got to the punch line.

I figured it out eventually. Koke and A.K. gave me some pointers, and although I wasn't all that experienced then, I had learned to watch what other fishermen were doing—especially the ones who were catching trout. It turned out to be a long, downstream drift and a fly pattern I didn't have: a size 12, extended body, Swisher and Richards Paradrake. Up until the moment I ran over to Mike Lawson's shop to buy a big handful of them, I'd have told you this was an ostentatious fly tied only to catch fishermen.

A.K. and I fished that hatch for a few more seasons, but I haven't been back to the Henry's Fork in over a dozen years now. The river has gone through some changes in that time, so I don't know if that fly still works or not. When a fly gets too popular on a heavily fished stream, it can sometimes wear itself out in a few seasons. But it's okay. There are so many tiers that there's always this year's hot new pattern, not to mention the nearby fly shop that can sell you a few.

I've also seen it happen that years after the old fly falls out of fashion, it begins to work again, probably because the fish that had learned to avoid it have all died off and you're now casting to a new generation of trout. And of course there are always those guys who do just fine, against the odds, with something like a big Adams.

There's a nice Green Drake hatch on the Frying Pan River in Colorado that some friends and I fished for quite a few years, and the fishing was a lot different there. Where the Henry's Fork on the Railroad Ranch and at Last Chance is smooth and lazy like a spring creek, the Pan is steep and rough. I won't say the fish were easier to catch, but in a lot of that water they didn't have much time to study a fly pattern, so at least the flies didn't have to be quite so anatomically correct.

On the other hand, the casting problems could be tremendous in water with so many conflicting currents, and of course a big, muscular trout in a fast river can take you for a quick ride and then leave you heartbroken. You have to think, Well, at least I hooked the son of a bitch.

We always did well with A.K.'s Frying Pan Green Drakes with their thick hackles and the oversized wings that make them flop in the water when the wind blows, just like the real bugs. But then sometimes Roy Palm's Hair-winged Drake worked best, and in quieter spots I sometimes had to go to a slightly fancy divided-wing parachute or even an emerger. And—it should go without saying—there were times when I couldn't get them on anything.

The best thing about this hatch is that it seems to go on forever: six weeks or even more in a good year. And then sometimes weeks or even a month after the hatch seems to be over, you'll still see a Drake on the water now and then—usually bumbling around in a fleet of Blue-winged Olives or Pale Morning Duns. The trout are used to seeing them by then and they know what they are, so it's possible to fish a Drake as a search pattern and pick up some fish.

Some of the sweetest Green Drake hatches I've fished have been in those small, nameless (by request) headwater creeks in British Columbia. These are narrow, rugged, a little remote, crawling with grizzly bears, and they hold wild, native west slope cutthroats. The best of these creeks have been described as like some waters in New Zealand where there aren't a lot of fish, but the ones that *are* there are almost all big.

The Drake hatches can be as sparse as the trout populations, and in another kind of water they could go almost unnoticed by the trout. But in these small, freestone creeks where food can be scarce, the fish get on the big mayflies like there was no tomorrow.

You hike from pool to pool—which is sometimes a long way— and you usually get one shot at a great big cutthroat rising in a clear, slow run. You want the fish desperately, so the pressure is on anyway, and constantly looking over your shoulder for bears doesn't help to steady your nerves. (One night I was so jumpy that when I got back to my motel room I had to look under the bed before I could turn in. It was doubtful that a griz could squeeze under there, but it didn't hurt to check.) Still, this is where you can get your twenty-inch or better wild cutt on a dry fly, and it seems worth risking a nervous breakdown to do it.

The Green Drake hatch on a little spring creek in Alberta was sweet, but it was a nightmare to fish. The trout were big and eager enough, but the stream was slow and smooth, muddy-bottomed and deep, with vertical banks and a jungle of willow all around it. The ground was muskeg that bounced like a wet mattress, and a heavy footfall on the bank could send ripples into the stream fifteen feet away.

Your approach had to be stealthy, your cast long and quiet. I remember torpedo-shaped wakes flushing ahead of me. I remember casts that would have been flawless if I hadn't hooked the willows behind me. I caught almost all my fish in the few easy places. Thank God there were some easy places.

One day I fished with a local named George, who I was happy to see was having some of the same troubles I was. During a break I asked him about some rumors I'd heard of grizzly bears along this stream. I won't say I was nervous, but you couldn't see ten feet through those willows and you couldn't run ten steps if your life depended on it.

George smiled at his boots and said, "The only grizzly bears I know of are the ones I made up to scare people away."

And then just last summer, Chris, Vince, and I fished a great Green Drake hatch on a small river in Wyoming. Chris guides out of a fly shop just over the state line in northern Colorado and he knows the area well. (The shop's motto is "If your friends don't fly-fish, get new friends.") Vince and I had fished farther up in the headwaters, but we'd never been on this particular stretch of river before, although there was some urgency about the trip. We'd been hearing about this hatch for a season or two, and if we'd heard about it in another state, it meant it was out of the bag and a Web site couldn't be far behind. The one drawback to Green Drake hatches is, the good ones draw fishermen like flies.

There's a public section of less than a mile at the upper end of this stretch, and then several miles of private water; seriously private and posted in the threatening, no-nonsense way Wyoming ranchers have perfected. But under state law you can float the water as long as you don't get out on the bank, set foot on the bottom, or drop an anchor. Technically, you might be in trouble if your raft bumped a rock, but I'd take that one all the way to the Supreme Court.

There are stories of confrontations on this river: cowboys on the dirt road honking their horns and giving fishermen the finger, rocks being thrown, that kind of thing. There are also vague rumors of darker stuff: probably not true, but you have to think they might be. Still, you're legally in the right, the river is good enough to be worth the trouble, and, honestly, I'd much rather face a pissed-off human than an even mildly irritated grizzly bear.

We dawdled around on the public water in the morning, wade-fishing and casting caddis flies to the occasional rising trout until the Green Drakes started to come off. Chris, who's done this dozens of times, didn't want to waste any of the precious water downstream by floating through it before the hatch started.

By then the Drakes had already been hatching for a couple of weeks, so as soon as the big mayflies started showing themselves in mid-morning, the fish immediately got on them. Trout love Green Drakes, probably just because they're big enough to make for an easy meal, although the fish get so eager you have to think they also taste good.

Anyway, we each hooked a few fish on Drake patterns in the public water, then piled into Chris's little twelve-foot raft and headed downstream past the biggest no trespassing sign I've ever seen. It was actually more like a billboard that explained the rules and what would happen if you broke them, all in painful detail. Chris said, "If anyone has to pee, do it now, 'cause we can't get out later."

The river was almost too low, even for the small raft, but Chris is a good boatman, and he managed to squeeze through neatly except for one minor boat wreck when we tried to go over a diversion dam. As we came up on it, Chris said it looked worse than it was; that at the bottom of the twelve-foot high dam we'd just shoot out straight like you would off the lip of a slide. But apparently the water was a little deeper the last time he tried this (or the guy in the bow was a little lighter), because at the bottom of the dam we stopped dead at a 45-degree angle and ended up in a pile. There were no casualties, though; not even a broken fly rod. Just a big, collective "Oof."

There's always a wrinkle, and here it's stream flow. This is not a big river, and for the last half of most seasons it's too low to float in even the smallest, most forgiving raft. The Green Drakes usually come right on the cusp of that, so you squeeze down it in the smallest possible boat, illegally bumping midstream rocks.

When the water starts dropping, Chris will drive a stake right at the water line at the put-in, and the next morning he'll compare today's flow with yesterday's float. He'll meditate on his stick for a few seconds while you hold your breath, waiting for him to say, "Yeah, we can do this."

The hatch lasted for hours that day, pumping up when the sky clouded over—which was most of the time—and then petering off a little when the sun came out. Trout were rising in all the likely places and for once there was no mystery about it. Big heads were bulging the surface and big duns with tall wings were going down in the swirls. No masking hatches, no crippled duns or floating emergers. It was a storybook Green Drake hatch.

I was fishing my divided-wing parachute Drake flies. These things are effective as hell—if I do say so myself—but they're also time consuming to tie and not as durable as some flies. I usually reserve them for the most difficult fish, but this was such a pretty hatch I thought it would be disrespectful to use anything but my prettiest flies.

For the few hours the hatch was at its best, we caught lots of trout, mostly rainbows, but also a few browns and the odd cut-throat. Many of them were around a foot long, but a lot were bigger. The best one we got was a rainbow that measured twenty-one inches, but probably half the trout we caught were over sixteen, and we could only wonder about the ones we couldn't land.

And you're right: Sizes and numbers aren't all of it by a long shot, but that's the easiest part to talk about without getting all mushy. And anyway, the paradox of storytelling is that when things go perfectly, there's not much to say.

The first time you hit a hatch this good, you wish it was like this every day, but pretty soon you begin to see that it can't be and probably shouldn't be. If there were much more than an outside chance of success, you'd quickly become bored with fishing and start playing the stock market. In the long run, fishing usually amounts to a lifetime of pratfalls punctuated by rare moments of perfection. When you're in the middle of one of those moments, all you can do is to shoot for grace and humility and try not to become hysterical. On the best day of fishing you'll ever have, you still won't be able to catch them all.

The hatch shut down in late afternoon, and we rode the rest of the way out without casting, just watching birds and enjoying the canyon. I suppose we could have picked up a few more fish on cad-dis flies, but what would have been the point of that?

In one long stretch we went through a dark cloud of mosquitoes bad enough that to make these seem better I had to mediate on the places where they'd been worse: Alaska, Labrador, a little stream flowing through a hay meadow in Colorado. This usually becomes a nice little reverie, since most of the places where I've been memorably pestered by mosquitoes were also those where I caught big fish.

Meditation can be made to work for short periods of time, but when the bugs settle in and begin to seem permanent, you have to think that if caribou can be driven so insane by these things that they'll stampede blindly for thirty miles, why should you be any different?

There are days when I'll still be casting even as the boat is within yards of the takeout, but after an especially good day I like to sit for the last half hour or so and enjoy the ride. (At first I had to force myself to do that. Now it comes more naturally.) I might be cold or tired, maybe I'm enduring some mosquito bites, but I almost always manage a feeling of self-satisfaction: the kind where I can glance quickly at life—ignoring many troublesome details—and think, I have accomplished everything I set out to do, even though I didn't set out to do much.

At the end of this float, you pop out of the little canyon onto a larger river, and all the extra sky is a surprise. You also drift away from that cloud of mosquitoes, although you'll run into them again a mile down river at the takeout. At the end of a normal day, there'll be a dozen or more boats coming off the main river in the evening, and it's feeding time for the bugs, so everyone is being very quick and efficient about trailering up the boats and getting the hell out of there.

As we were taking the raft out, a fisherman walked over and asked Chris how we'd done. He picked Chris because he was clearly the one in charge, but the guy couldn't have known that he's one of those soft-spoken fishing guides who can occasionally raise vagueness to the level of an art form. Chris said, "Oh, we just had a nice day on the river." Never mind which river, never mind how good a day. It was true enough without giving anything away.

Chapter 18

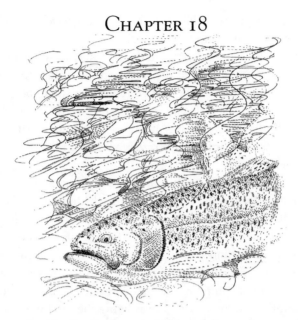

It was late in September and Ed and I were camped on the Frying Pan River near Basalt, Colorado, for the better part of a week. The regular campsite there is in a small, open stand of narrow-leaf cottonwoods about thirty yards from the river on some property owned by our friend Roy Palm. It's roughly halfway between town and Ruedi Dam, on a long bend in the river. If you look upstream from camp, you see the Continental Divide above Hagerman Pass. In the other direction you see forested slopes on one side of the river and bare rust-colored hematite cliffs on the other. Farther downstream those rocks loom up fantastically into a formation known as the Seven Castles, and below that is the Seven Castles Pool: a long, wide, glassy nightmare that's said to be the toughest pool on the river. I remember it being tough. I threw up my hands there eight or ten years ago and haven't fished it since.

This grove of trees is where everyone camps when they visit Roy—and Roy has a lot of fishing friends because for decades he's been a guide, fly tier, fly shop owner, and all-around outdoor wild man. If you fly-fish, live in Colorado, and are of a certain age and inclination, you probably know Roy and may have shared some hangovers with him back in your reckless youth.

This is the cleanest campsite you're ever likely to see. Aside from a fire ring a safe distance from the trees and the neat remnants of a firewood pile, you'd never be able to tell that a single person had camped there, let alone dozens of people over the years. Either none of Roy's friends are slobs, or they at least realize that, as generous as their host is, a pile of garbage would mean they'd never get to camp there again.

That year there was a pretty good supply of seasoned oak firewood left over from a guide who lived back there in a tent for a while. He has since gone on to one of the places people living in tents eventually go; in this case, to a job, a house, and a wife far from the river, leaving behind a dwindling stack of good hardwood that Ed and I happily burned for cooking and warmth. One or two more cold-weather camps and it'll all be gone, along with the last traces of another young guy who was living the life for a while.

Ed and I usually pitch tents here, but on this trip we slept under the camper shells on our pickups because of the bear situation. The hot, dry summer had driven hundreds of black bears down out of the high country to search for food, and by September they were wandering the streets of mountain and foothills towns, eating gardens and raiding garbage cans and campgrounds.

It was annoying and potentially dangerous for humans, but, as usual, the bears were worse off. A two-hundred-pound black bear has to put on another eighty pounds in the fall to be in good shape for hibernation, and some of these hungry animals were destined to go to sleep and never wake up.

We took the normal precautions of keeping the camp even cleaner than usual, barricading our food and garbage in the cabs of the trucks, and sleeping in something with hard sides. (Of course, an adult black bear can open an aluminum camper shell like a sardine can, but at least you'll have more warning than you would in a flimsy nylon tent.) Apparently we did okay, because one night Roy had a bear sniffing around his cabin, but it either didn't notice our camp a hundred yards away, or it did but couldn't find anything it wanted.

Naturally, we ended up telling a few bear stories around the fire at night. All fishermen have bear stories—whether or not they've ever actually seen a bear—and they'll tell them at the slightest provocation. I dragged out my current favorite because Ed hadn't heard it yet. It was told to me by a man I know from China: the acupuncturist who cured my nagging case of fly caster's elbow with needles and herbs.

He said that in the mountains of his home province, bears would sometimes sneak up behind hikers and tap them on the shoulder. The locals knew that if you ignored the tap and kept walking, the bears would leave you alone, but if you turned around to see what it was, they'd probably kill you.

Then he gazed out the window and said, "It is very hard not to turn around."

At first I thought this trip would be all about changing gears. The Pan is a tailwater fishery known as a very technical river. Now and then I have to explain to nonfishermen that "technical" is the euphemism we use when we mean it's just plain hard to catch the fish. Sometimes they reply, "Well then, why don't you just *say* that?"

I had somehow managed to get all the way into September having fished a tailwater exactly once—one day on the South Platte River back in April, where I caught a few nice rainbows on a sparse Blue-winged Olive hatch—so I was out of practice on the difficult stuff.

There had been a few trips through the season and not all the fishing was easy, but mostly I'd been fishing the freestone creeks close to home, often dealing with trout that were hungry and aggressive and not particularly selective. Not to brag or anything, but I was pretty much death from above on easy fish.

I'd been fishing a lot, too. It had been a god-awful hot summer. We'd broken the all-time record for days that got to ninety degrees or more, wildfires burned, wild berry crops failed, and herds of hungry bears were pouring out of the mountains. Once this would have just been miserable but temporary. Now it was too easy to get into a righteous funk about global warming. This can take all kinds of forms, including the urge to fish like hell now, before all the trout streams have boiled away.

But in spite of all that, my life was going pretty much the way I wanted it to for once. I was working a little in the cool mornings, and then in the afternoons, when the heat settled in and I started to wilt, I'd drive up into the hills, wade wet in an ice-cold trout stream and catch some fish. Even in that dry western heat, my wading boots were often still damp from the day before.

So, although I didn't exactly have stage fright, I did wonder how long it would take me to get back into the tailwater thing: the multiple hatches; the meticulous drifts and fly changes; the trout that are so snooty they've been known to refuse even the naturals late in the season. For months my fishing had been casual—possibly even sloppy—and I couldn't remember the last time I'd used a dry fly smaller than a size 14. I could, however, remember that failure at fishing feels like a slow-motion train wreck, and I guess I was honestly afraid of it.

As it turned out, all it took was about half an hour on the first hatch and the two fly boxes I hadn't looked into all summer—the ones with the size 18 and smaller midges and mayflies. Of course, there are plenty of fishermen who are better at this—including Ed and Roy—but I hooked some trout and didn't break all of them off of those unfamiliar 6 and 7x tippets.

The definitive kick in fly-fishing is that moment when things fall together—when and *if* they fall together. There's an ineffable quality to it, but once you get past the amazement, it feels comfortably familiar.

Once, sometime in the 1960s, I went to my first Grateful Dead concert. At first I didn't get it. The band was up on stage honking away in an uninspired way, while the people in the audience were talking, reading, napping, playing Frisbee, and conducting certain shady-looking transactions. I wondered what was going on. The Dead were supposed to be great and their concerts were known to go for many hours and be life-changing. I considered leaving, but then I'd either paid good money to get in or climbed a perfectly good chain-link fence, so I stuck it out.

Then, maybe an hour into the performance, something just clicked. I couldn't tell you what it was, but I recognized it as if it happened every day: The band was playing brilliantly, the audience put away its books and Frisbees, and a few thousand of us were kicking out the jams, as we used to say. The hatch had started, the trout were rising, and everyone had the right fly.

That night in camp I said to Ed, "You know, it all came back to me pretty quickly." He said something like, "Yeah, it's nice to just know what you're doing, isn't it?" and it occurred to me that a fishing trip is one of the few times when I not only know what I'm doing, but also what I'm *supposed* to be doing. Maybe that's why I spend so much time on the water.

Looking back on it, I don't know why I was worried except maybe that's just what we do. We know that having done it before—even hundreds of times before—doesn't automatically mean we can do it again, so we have to find out, and that's what keeps us fishing.

When I was a kid, I wanted to grow up to be one of those calm, unflappable outdoorsmen; you know, those gray-haired guys in beat-up hats who were never surprised and who never panicked. I have the hair and the hat now, but otherwise I'm still fourteen years old, and I suspect they were, too: masters of stillness on the outside, festering shitholes of uncertainty just under the surface.

It rained one night—it sounded like hammers on the camper shell—but mostly it was crisp and sunny, and that pushed the hatches into the mornings and evenings and left slow middays with few fish rising. I didn't mind that because I like a slow-paced trip late in the season and also because it was comfortable weather to be out in, but the awful heat was over, so I no longer had to contemplate The End at least once every day.

One afternoon we got a wild hair and drove down the Frying Pan, on down the Roaring Fork, and then back up the Crystal

River past the little town of Redstone, where a feeder creek was coming in muddy. We went over there because the Crystal is a free-stone stream where trout might eat a dry fly in the middle of a sunny day and because neither of us had ever fished it.

We spent a few hours potting around in some pocket water, catching rainbows from ten to thirteen inches on big dry flies. They were stockers, but the bigger ones were probably holdovers from previous years. They were fat and pretty, they jumped, and they just generally acted wild, even to being sort of stupid.

We were back in camp by three, getting ready for the evening rise when Roy wandered out and asked us how we'd done that day. We told him and he said, "Jeez, you mean you went and caught those god-damn stockers when you have *this*?" He made an expansive gesture that took in the entire Frying Pan Valley. I don't think he was actually mad at us, but he may have been a little disappointed. I tried to look ashamed of myself.

That evening we had a multiple hatch that started with Saratelas, then went on to Blue-winged Olives, Pale Morning Duns, Sulphur Duns, and Sulphur Spinners, plus a scattering of small caddis flies and even the odd Green Drake: the last of a hatch that had started seven weeks ago. I kept up with it pretty well with only one hint from Ed.

I said, "They don't like my emerger anymore."

He said, "Look at the fish. That's a spinner rise."

Ed is not someone you want to compare yourself to on a tailwater. He's fished these things for years, guided on them successfully, and has written a good book about them that's called, in his typical, straightforward way, *Fly Fishing the Tailwaters.* He's also a good caster, a strong wader, and a fine observer, but beyond all that he has the quality Tom McGuane once called "smoothness." It's hard to describe. He doesn't seem to be doing anything special, but he's fishing circles around you. Eventually you get used to it.

After years of fishing this river, we had a pretty good idea of where to look for rising trout, and we knew at least some of the places where the bigger ones have been known to lie. We also had the flies we like for the regular hatches, with the exception of the

Saratelas. This is a strange and rare mayfly that probably exists else-where, but that I've never seen or heard of anywhere but on the Pan. Roy, who's studied the bugs and consulted entomologists, says they're hermaphroditic, flightless, and they're born pregnant. I thought it was the opening line of a joke, but he was serious. He's the only fisherman I know who can predictably catch fish during this hatch, and even *he* says he doesn't have it wired yet.

By then I was on a pretty good roll. Sometimes I spend the first hours of a fishing trip with my mind racing about what I didn't do before I left, what I'll have to do when I get back, and what I should do, but won't, and will end up feeling guilty about. At its worst, this can degenerate into the old if-this-then-what? kind of business where I end up worrying about things that haven't hap-pened and probably never will. Naturally, all that causes me to tie on the wrong fly and then cast it to the wrong place.

But at some point (and the sooner the better) I remember that for years now all that stuff has either waited patiently for me to get home or it has taken care of itself one way or another in my absence, so the hell with it. Then I'm just fishing and now and then thinking—as all fishermen have thought from time to time—I am the last sane person on earth.

Another afternoon, after a nice morning midge hatch near camp, we were driving up the river with no particular place in mind when we passed a good stretch of water that's usually crowded but was weirdly vacant that day. We decided to fish there for no other reason than that we could.

There were a few odd bugs around, but no rising fish, so I tried working the likely looking spots with a #14 Elk Hair Caddis and a #16 Hare's Ear Soft Hackle behind it on a dropper—the same kind of nondescript, freestone sort of rig I'd been fishing for much of the summer. I got two small browns on the dry and one pretty good rainbow on the dropper. It was good to see the old trick work, even on the famously technical Frying Pan.

This piece of water is known as "Old Faithful" because if you can't catch a fish on a dry fly anywhere else on the river, you can sometimes catch one here, but I can't help thinking of it as the Grave of the Unknown Fisherman because of the plaque. It's fastened to a big, lichen-covered rock above the river, and it reads:

> INSTREAM HABITAT WORK
> DONE WITH FUNDS
> PROVIDED BY FRIENDS AND FAMILY
> IN MEMORY OF
> KENNETH HUTCHINS
> AN AVID FISHERMAN

There's something to be learned about brevity from the language of plaques. Can you adequately sum up a man's entire life just by saying he was an avid fisherman? Well, I think you could mine.

Chapter 19

I t was only a few weeks after the Frying Pan trip that Vince, Chris, Mike Clark, and I were floating the North Platte River in Wyoming. According to the weather maps, there was a low-pressure front approaching slowly from the northwest, and the plan was to slip in under it for the last day or two of good weather and the hot fishing that can come on a falling barometer. Of course, some fishing trips are almost preordained disasters, but you learn to love them as good yarns in the making or occasions for feeling heroic—the things that keep you from giving up fishing for something tamer and more comfortable.

We always make this float late in the season; October or even early November. It can still be gorgeous then, but Wyoming weather is more of a gamble the later it gets. Still, the season is winding down, so there are few other boats on the river, and the streamer fishing for big rainbows can be magnificent if you hit it right—although you can really *not* hit it right.

Mostly we do it then because Chris finally has some free time after a full summer and fall of guiding fishermen. He fishes a little himself on these floats, but usually he just rows and enjoys having friends in the boat who can cast well enough and who aren't paying him. It took me a long time to realize that for some guides—some of the best, anyway—this is a good day off: doing for free what they normally do for a living. Over the years I have seen this cause people to go off alone to ponder the nature of their own jobs.

Anyway, we launched the two drift boats in the morning and had a slow time of it for a few hours. The flow was right, but the water was a little off-color, a little too cold, and the day seemed too bright. A few trout were caught on streamers (Mike got a nice big brown), and Vince and I beached his boat on a sandbar and teased a few fish that were halfhalfheartedly rising to Blue-winged Olives, but that was about it. As it turned out, the barometer would have been falling about then, but apparently these trout were immune to it.

Then, late in the morning, the wind picked up, the air got chilly, and the sky turned gray. We'd seen it coming from a distance and thought maybe it would just cloud up and shade the water, but at the last minute it seemed to pounce on us. Someone said, "Well, here's that front."

An hour later it was near freezing, dark as evening, and the wind was howling upstream. We'd squeezed into all the clothing we'd brought and it wasn't enough. The two guys at the oars—Chris and Vince—were pulling hard trying to make headway downstream into the wind. It was a struggle, even with the current trying to help. Mike and I kept casting for a while, but our hands froze and there were no fish, so we finally gave it up.

Then it was just about getting off the river. We had six miles to go to the take-out against a freezing gale that would blow the boats back upstream if we stopped rowing. I was very cold hunkered in the bow with my back to the wind. I asked Vince if he wanted me to spell him on the oars.

He said, "No, I'm okay."

I said, "I could use the exercise to keep warm."

He said, "Really, I'm okay."

He outweighs me by more than sixty pounds and it's his boat. I damn near froze to death.

There was nothing left to do but watch the scenery. It was low and rolling, dark, mostly treeless, but with stands of bare cottonwoods, willows, and dogwoods along the water; all of it going by way too slowly. Tucked under sheltered banks, a few lonesome ducks were looking miserable, or at least bored. If there's a trout stream on the dark side of the moon, this is what it looks like.

We ate well that night—or at least we ate a lot—and slept dry and warm at a Super 8 Motel. The next morning before dawn, we straggled down to the lobby for the free coffee and looked out at the parking lot. It was snowing horizontally. The boats were covered and almost unrecognizable. We all made the obligatory noises about going out anyway or waiting to see if it cleared off, but it was just that ritual whereby no one wants to be the first one to pull the plug.

On the long, slow drive home through a near-blizzard, Chris and I stopped to check out a van that had flipped upside down on the side of the icy road. You do this because you have to, but I remember thinking, Don't let me see something I won't be able to forget. But it was okay. There was no one inside and no blood. And there were tracks in the fresh snow where two people had gotten out, walked back up to the road under their own power, and flagged a ride.

At Laramie both roads south were closed by drifting snow. We had lunch in a cafe crowded with truck drivers. Then we hung out at the Laramie Fly Shop until the clerks started to get suspicious. Then we went to the Pioneer Museum, where we saw a neat bearskin overcoat and a set of snowshoes for horses. Mike, who was a cowboy four or five careers ago, said they'd never work.

When they finally opened the pass over to Virginia Dale, we ground off behind a line of eighteen-wheelers and talked about the last time we'd hit the North Platte right: the cool, comfortable day and all those big trout so hungry for streamers. When you talk about it, it always goes right, even though your true memories are full of storms.

. . .

For the most part, though, float-fishing is a downright luxurious way to fish. If you're casting, you're being chauffeured down a big river to within range of all kinds of good water you'd never be able to fish by wading, even if you were a tournament caster. You soon learn that you can't fish everywhere, but you can fish *any*where.

If you're rowing, you're in charge in a small, democratic way. You don't ignore suggestions, but if no one says anything, you pick the route. The better you are as a boatman, the better the fishing goes. You feel that responsibility, so you're always thinking and then thinking ahead.

On your first few floats you might make the same beginners' mistakes I made, like forgetting that the boat is moving, casting straight at the passing bank and getting instant drag. Maybe you apply the laws of physics and figure it out for yourself, or maybe a helpful guide has to point out that you should cast steeply downstream ahead of the boat so you'll get a longer drift.

If you're in the bow, casting downstream will also give your partner in the stern some room to fish. He'll appreciate that, and on days when justice prevails, he'll return the favor when you switch seats at lunchtime.

The bow seat in a drift boat is naturally the best position because you come to everything first, but it's only right to pass up half the really fishy-looking spots so your partner in the back can have a shot at some water you haven't already pounded. You'll also fish better if you take your time and don't get greedy. From a moving drift boat, the obvious spots to fish are like targets in a shooting gallery. They all look so good and they go by so fast. You can seriously lose it trying to cast to all of them.

The common accident in a drift boat with two fly casters is tangled lines. Usually it's minor and just takes a little unsnarling, but I've seen rods broken and people slapped in the face with hooks, too. It helps if you can keep both casts going at the same angle, but it's even better to alternate casts, with one line on the water while the other is in the air.

It's the fisherman in the stern who usually has to watch the timing of the casts because the guy in front has his back to the rest of the boat and he's probably oblivious anyway. At its best, this just demands a little peripheral attention, but it becomes crucial if one of the fishermen in the boat is casting with what Mel Krieger calls "the salmon egg sling."

Tangles aside, you'll come up against some interesting casting problems in a drift boat. The range and the angle of the drift change constantly, and as often as not you'll get only one good shot from the moving boat. You learn to divide your attention; fishing out one cast while mentally setting up for the next. And of course trout have an uncanny way of eating your fly in the exact split second it takes you to glance downstream to the next pocket. This can be a lot to think about, so it naturally works best if you can do it *without* thinking.

Once, on a float down the Old Man River in Alberta, Vince casually asked me, "How do you suppose we can have the ranges always changing like this, but still be able to shoot line and hit the right spot as often as we do?" He's a casting instructor, so he worries about these things, which is fine for him, but I got to pondering it myself and couldn't cast for the next hour. At lunch I said, "Don't you ever say anything like that to me again, you hear?"

And then there's line handling. After the first twenty minutes of shooting line for long casts and then stripping it in for short ones, you'll have yards of fly line on the deck at your feet and you'll almost surely be standing on some of it. If you're in the bow, it's possible to use the foredeck as a casting apron, but my line always wants to snake off and either slide overboard or at least hook one of the horns of the leg brace.

Like almost everything else in fishing, the more you fish from a drift boat, the more neatly it all falls together until one day you realize you're not half bad at this. Then there's the inevitable day when you get a little cocky and pay for it in front of witnesses. You finally start to get good when you quit trying to show off.

In some ways you set your own pace on a float, and in others the river sets it for you. Most of the North Platte is pretty placid by

Rocky Mountain standards and can be taken slowly. The local ins and outs include stretches of private land where you're not supposed to get out and wade or even drop the anchor. They're marked by small blank signs nailed to trees: red for private land, blue for public. There's no writing at all, so if you're not in on it, you don't have a clue what they could mean.

The Elk River in British Columbia is more brawling and pockety, and fishing from the boat is usually fast paced and even a little frantic. But then you stop and wade-fish enough good pools, runs, and side channels to break that up, although never as many as you'd like to.

On most of these floats, you'll go by dozens of long, fishy runs that you'd spend at least half an hour on if you were wading, but where you'll have to satisfy yourself with one or two quick drifts as the boat goes by. When you blow a cast on a spot like that, you mourn a little but recover quickly because here comes the next one. It's part of the deal, because to some extent you have to keep moving or you'll end up rowing out in the dark, which is no fun even on familiar water.

At first I thought rowing a drift boat couldn't be that hard. I mean, the current is moving you downstream anyway, so all you have to do is steer, right? But the first few times I tried it were successful only insofar as I got the boat down the river without hitting either bank. The fishermen I was rowing were friends and didn't say anything, but I could see the shoulders of the guy in the bow slump every time I set up wrong and ran over a pod of rising trout. I came to appreciate the skill of the good guides I'd fished with who made it look easy.

I've gotten better at it with practice. I'll never be as good as the people who pull oars for a living, but I can now set up properly more often than not, and I can often do it far enough in advance that all it takes is a few lazy dips of the oars instead of a desperate last-minute correction. The floats I like best now are the ones where I get to row about half the time.

The best boatmen I've seen are the ones who seem to work the least, quietly chopping an oar here and there and always coming up on a spot at the right place, with the boat cocked at just the angle that lets both fishermen get off a good cast. They're using style instead of brute force and also saving themselves for, say, the eddy with the huge trout rising. This is where you want to put your back into it and stop the boat dead in the current for the space of two, three, maybe four casts. It should be a big fish, and your sport should say thanks whether he hooks it or not.

But most of the time—when it's done well—drift-fishing is like a slow toboggan slide, or a leaf drifting down the current, or a sixteen-foot fiberglass dry fly on a ten-mile drag-free float with a stop for lunch and a couple of piss breaks. It's not always effortless, even for the best oarsmen, but it can be made to look that way.

If you go on enough floats that go well, you can begin to think there's very little that can go wrong, but in fact there's plenty.

Wind can be a problem on western rivers. Sometimes it's a minor annoyance, other times it's a daylong struggle. Either way, the wind pushes you one way, the current nudges you another, and nine times out of ten you're trying to row somewhere in between. The standard procedure is to put your back into the wind and row against it at the same rate it's pushing against you, thereby canceling out its effects. It sounds easy enough in theory, but, as Chris once said, in practice it's like trying to stand on a basketball.

And there are always rocks to hit. Usually it's nothing—a little bump and a scratch in the finish—but even moderate currents are powerful and relentless, so once the wrong thing starts to happen, it will go on happening until it reaches its own inevitable conclusion.

I once saw a drift boat capsize on the Henry's Fork in Idaho: the only time I've seen one actually go over. There was a long, slow bend that dropped into those rapids just above Osborne Bridge. The guide may have been unfamiliar with the river or he may have been distracted by something like changing one of his client's flies, but he went into the fast water sideways, hit a rock in the main current, and the boat turned on its side. From where A.K. and I were wading fifty yards downstream, it seemed to happen slowly, so I couldn't understand why all three people flew out. Maybe it was an optical illusion, or maybe they jumped.

A.K. and I waded out quickly and managed to save an oar and a cooler, but most of the gear was lost, including some expensive fly rods. Everyone survived, but the guide was deeply embarrassed and the clients were mad as wet hens. It could have been much worse.

I once met a guide in Canada who also had a bad one. He was scouting a canyon stretch that was pretty rough, but it was in a decent flow and he knew it well, so it should have been only an exciting ride. But there'd been a landslide he didn't know about, so there was a brand-new thirty-foot waterfall that he came on suddenly and couldn't help but go over. There wasn't even time to set up on it, although exactly *how* you'd set up on something like that I'm not sure. "Thought I was fuckin' dead," he said.

I was with this guy a few seasons later in the same canyon. He had an ancient, high-sided, wooden McKenzie boat that didn't look very seaworthy, and someone asked him, "Why'd you bring that old tub?"

The guy said, "Didn't want to bust up the good boat in here."

Comments like that can make me think twice about getting in the boat, but then there I am, with waders on and rod in hand, so I get in the boat anyway, figuring maybe it was all just a story. Some guides like to scare their clients a little. It makes them more docile and obedient.

If you're a real guide instead of a guy taking his turn at the oars among friends, you quickly learn that the hardest part of rowing a drift boat isn't the rowing, it's dealing with the clients. Getting the boat down the river is one thing, but apparently it's quite another when you also have to conduct a daylong casting lesson, stop every five minutes to untangle leaders and tie on flies, and deal with all manner of strange and unique screwups.

Every guide has stories about bumbling duffers: It's part of the lore of the profession. I always believed those stories, but I never got the full effect until I saw one for myself. I was in a boat with Chris and another fisherman. He was a stranger to both of us, and how he ended up in the boat that day is a long story that I won't tell because it doesn't matter. The point is, it became obvious within the first ten minutes that although the guy had talked a good game on shore, he didn't know how to cast. I don't mean to say he wasn't very good, I mean he had no idea how to do it.

His casting arc covered well over one hundred eighty degrees, so that both his line and his rod tip splashed the water on the forward and back casts. As hard as he tried—and he put every ounce of strength he had into it—he couldn't get the fly past the oars. I'd heard it said of poor casters that they whipped the water to a froth, but I'd never actually seen it done before.

So Chris began to explain the basic mechanics of fly casting in a quiet, patient voice: the brisk back cast, the stop just past your ear with the rod tip pointing up and slightly back, the hesitation to let the line straighten out, and then the deliberate but gentle forward cast.

The guy splashed the water hard behind and in front, and his fly landed predictably just under the rod tip. He said, "Yeah, that makes a big difference."

To make a long story short, the poor guy either couldn't or wouldn't get it. Chris tried long, detailed explanations, then the shortest ones possible, like "Don't bend your wrist." The guy continued to lash the water, never got his fly much more than a rod's length from the boat, and of course never hooked a fish. The guides Chris hangs out with have a code for clients like this: O.S.B. It means, "Other Sports Beckon."

Chris would let him flail around for a while and then try another approach, even though he was clearly running out of different ways to explain the same thing. An objective observer would have said he was as patient five hours into the float as he'd been in the beginning, but if you were there to see the whole thing unfold you'd have realized that he was getting *too* patient—ominously patient, you might say.

At one point I wondered if maybe some joker hadn't paid this guy a hundred dollars to stage this performance, but I dismissed that. No one I know is quite that cruel.

Finally, two-thirds of the way through the day, Chris slipped the boat into a quiet backwater, stood up, and said, "Okay! That's it!"

I thought he was going to break the guy's rod over his knee or maybe even throw him in the river (I'd have done both hours ago), but instead he dug a roll of adhesive tape out of his first aid kit and roughly taped the butt of the man's rod to his forearm just below the wrist. Then he looked the guy straight in the eye and said, in a barely controlled voice, "Don't. Bend. Your. Wrist!"

To continue to splash the water behind him without bending his wrist, the guy had to almost bend over backwards, but he managed it, and within a few minutes his leader was badly snarled and he was sitting in his seat trying to pick it out.

We drifted on in silence for ten minutes or so, and the guy continued to sit with his back to us and his head down. (I'd given him the bow seat that morning to be polite. I let him keep it all day so I could keep an eye one him.) Finally Chris asked, "Having trouble getting that leader untangled?"

The guy said, "Well, it's not easy with a rod taped to your wrist."

I could tell by Chris's body language that he'd given up. He apologized, cut the man loose, and left him alone until we made it to the take-out.

Looking back, it must have been just another day on the river: the kind that has formed the mythology of guiding. Back in the 1940s, Ed Zern wrote, "In the evening, guides sit around the campfire and spit in it. They like to hear the sizzle. After a day of fishing, it makes sense."

The next morning we went out again, this time with one of Chris's old favorite clients who was a nice guy and a stylish caster. Trout were caught and once again life was good, but in some circles, this is now my claim to fame: I was there the day Mr. Mellow finally lost it.

But when it goes well—and it does go well often enough—rowing the boat and setting up your fishermen for good casts is as fine a skill as fishing itself and just as satisfying. (In a way, you *are* fishing: It's just that someone else is holding the rod.) At its very best, something sublime happens. Within the first half hour the boatman has learned that his fisherman can read water well enough, so he no longer has to say, "Good spot coming up on the left." He's also figured out how well the guy can cast, so he knows how close he has to get to where the fish are—or how far out he can stay. At the same time, the fisherman has gotten used to how the guy at the oars is going to set him up, so he can anticipate with some confidence and use the motion of the boat to get the last two feet on his cast.

It won't last forever, but while it does last there's no need for talk. The oarsman feels like he's casting, the caster feels like he's steering the boat, and beyond that there's just trout rising, birds singing, and the wind in your hair.

After doing it right a few times, you begin to see why guides say they "got their clients into fish" instead of just that they caught some.

CHAPTER 20

Anyone would go fishing thinking he'll catch something. It's when you go figuring you probably won't that you know you've crossed some kind of line. That's what winter fly-fishing can be about. I know it's possible to have glorious days in the winter—I've had a few—but for me, slow to completely blank days are much more common, and I've been a happier man since I've learned to live with that. Now I just go because I *can* go; because there's no closed season here in Colorado and the tailwaters usually stay open. It's also slightly less insane than some of the other things I've done out of desperation.

It's not like that with everyone, and it wasn't always like that with me, either. In the places where it's both legal and possible, winter fly-fishing can really get under the skin of a certain kind of fisherman. The most radical can almost get like those ice fishers who halfheartedly play golf all summer and fish only when they can walk out on the lakes pulling a sled.

Some like the solitude you can find on trout streams in winter. Frostbite fly-fishing has caught on over the years, but even now the difference between summer and winter crowds on famous rivers can be like night and day. It's still possible to have what seems like a whole river all to yourself, and even if you have company, there can be few enough of them that you'll want to stop and say hello.

There are also fishermen who like the macho aspects of it: You may be fishing tiny flies and a flimsy little rod, but by God it takes a real man to brave the elements.

And some are just amazed at open water and feeding trout at that time of year. At first I was a little surprised myself, but then I grew up in Minnesota, and once you've caught your first pike through the ice in the middle of a Minnesota winter, you'll never be completely astonished by anything ever again.

There was a time when some friends and I haunted the South Platte River in the winter, going down there as often as once a week between December and March. We'd usually walk into the Cheesman Canyon stretch that's nearest the dam and gets the full force of the tailwater effect, but sometimes we'd fish the roadside public water downstream of the Wigwam Club, especially on really cold days when we wanted to be close to the truck's heater.

In the canyon, we'd warm up with a fire made of willow twigs and a pot of boiled coffee. Some days, that's all winter fishing was: a two-and-a-half-hour drive, a thirty-minute hike, and a coffee break in waders. There were the great days when the trout were on midges and we caught lots of them, but winter fly-fishing has always been what you'd have to call spotty, and four out of five trips were either fishless or barely saved by one or two trout. It's not that we preferred winter—if September lasted all year, that would be fine with us. It's just that we needed to keep fishing because no one ever told us we couldn't.

Now our winter trips are more likely to be once a month than once a week, and they've slid forward in time. We'll start in mid-February because that's when the days get longer and the fishing begins to pick up. Then we'll fish occasionally through April when the Blue-winged Olives begin to appear and the fisherman's spring has officially arrived. Sometimes we kid each other about not being able to take the cold anymore, but in fact February and March can be our coldest, snowiest months, and even April can be uglier than winter.

We don't exactly have to force ourselves to go, but it's still easy *not* to go. Winter fly-fishing is one of those things you love but don't quite remember why when you're away from it. Descriptions of it sound exciting one minute and pointlessly uncomfortable the next. Photos of winter fly casters have the same effect. They're posed for extremes, with deep snow, maybe cross-country skis or snowshoes on the bank, maybe a dump of snow falling, fisherman bundled and hooded in arctic gear. You think, Now *that's* adventure. Then you think, Why not just move to Florida and fish for stump knockers off a dock? Well, because it's just possible that you could catch a trout. That's why not.

So when Mike Clark suggested we go ring in the new year on the Frying Pan River, I understood that he meant we'd stand up to our butts in ice-cold water for a couple of days on general principles. We'd fight the cold, fight the temptations of truck heaters and cozy cafes, and maybe we'd catch a fish.

It sounded okay. The float trip on the North Platte where we all nearly froze had been six weeks ago, and since then the fishing had seriously dropped off. As the season had wound down, one possibility after another was subtracted until it was down to a handful of tailwaters and a break from the weather. This happens predictably every year, but somehow it's still a surprise. Anyway, it had become the season where you go fly-fishing to prove to yourself that it's possible, but you haven't stopped waiting for spring.

I know Mike needed the break. He works longer and harder than most people think building bamboo fly rods for a living. (A common assumption is that people in the tackle business fish as much as they want to, but that's rarely true.) With his assistant Kathy Jensen doing the wraps, keeping the books, and answering the phone, and Mike doing just about everything else, he turns out something like forty new rods a year, plus a handful of restorations and repairs.

He works out of a small storefront on Main Street, so there are often lots of interruptions, and there's the inevitable tension between the way he sees himself—as a craftsman with steady work—and the way some of his clients see him—as artist, guru, and famous grouch.

In spring, summer, and fall Mike will fish, sometimes for a day or a week, sometimes just for an afternoon. You'll go down there and the place will be closed, with the GONE FISHING sign hanging in the window. Customers complain from time to time, but it does say, BY APPOINTMENT ONLY right there on the door. And anyway, you wouldn't want to buy a rod from a rod maker who doesn't fish, would you?

Like me, Mike tries to do as much work as possible through the winter so he can fish when the good fishing is there to do. Also like me, he can reach a point where the grind has gone on for too long.

We left at six-thirty in the morning, after breakfast at the Lyons Cafe, and big cups of road coffee at Mark's Off Broadway (formerly the Conoco station). We went through the usual motions: the four-hour drive over to Basalt—stopping at the usual place to pee and buy more coffee—checking into the Aspenalt Motel (where sometimes they remember us and sometimes they don't, but where they never mistake us for skiers), then checking in with Art at the Frying Pan Angler fly shop, where we bought our new licenses.

We'd tried to do that at home the day before, but there'd been a mixup at Ted's Hardware and, with January first just two days away, the new license book hadn't come in yet. So for the first time in over twenty years, we bought our resident fish and small game licenses someplace other than the local hardware store. I'm not especially superstitious—and it's only a piece of paper, after all—but I still couldn't help wondering if breaking the old routine could put a whammy on the whole season.

Finally we checked in with Roy Palm at his cabin up on the river. (Roy owns the fly shop, but he's seldom seen there.) He came to the door grinning and said he was glad to see us. "I'm getting the shack nasties," he said. "This time of year I only get an hour of sunlight up here." Then we sat down around the big, cluttered kitchen table and spent forty-five minutes catching up on things and petting the dogs. Hitting the river in mid-winter isn't the desperate business it is in warmer weather. There always seems to be time to talk things over and have another cup of coffee.

Down at the shop, Art had said there hadn't been much in the way of midge hatches lately, so we'd stand our best chance fishing small nymphs where the sun was on the water. Roy agreed, but said it wouldn't be easy finding a place like that up in the canyon with steep rock walls and the sun low in the sky. And then with the drive over and all the visiting, we had only a few hours left to fish before the sun was down, and it would be little or no use.

Naturally, the sun was not shining on the water in the places we wanted to fish, and there's more posted water than there used to be, so the choices are somewhat limited. Most of the signs just say NO FISHING, but a few have gotten downright nasty. Stepping off the road at an old familiar spot, it's possible to come on one that gets right in your face with IF YOU CAN READ THIS, YOU ARE TRESPASS-ING. *LEAVE NOW.* It's a brand-new sign with no bullet holes or added comments, but that's only a matter of time.

That sign is just downstream from a place known to local guides as the Moron's Pool because it's so easy to fish they can often take their most idiotic clients there and pull out an otherwise disastrous day. It was one of my favorite places to fish on that stretch of river until I learned what it was called. We went up there anyway. The sun was off it, and it looked pretty uninviting. We stood on a high bank and watched for a while, but the slot where the trout usually stack up looked empty.

In the little time we had left that day we found a spot that fit the profile: direct if fading sunlight on decent holding water, not posted, and no other fishermen. By dusk I'd hooked and lost a trout and Mike had actually landed a foot-long rainbow. The day was cold, but we were dressed for it and we weren't out long enough to get that creeping, bone-deep chill that takes hours to get rid of. It amounted to a fair to middling two hours of winter fly-fishing.

The next morning we drove down to a place near Cemetery Rapids on the Roaring Fork River, where we thought there'd be more sun on the river and warmer water, but the run was choked with chunks of ice and slush, and it was impossible to fish. Beautiful water, though, and a more open valley with lots of sunlight. We watched the ice floe for a while, knowing there were fish down there that we couldn't cast to no matter how much split shot we nipped onto our leaders. It seemed vaguely unfair.

So back up to the Frying Pan where, at about ten-thirty in the morning, the sun had just hit the water at a long pool called Rosie's. We dredged #22 nymphs in the head of the pool: tandem rigs in different combinations of patterns, mostly Pheasant Tails, Blue-winged Olive nymphs, and assorted midge pupae. No one pattern was clearly the answer, but eventually we caught a couple of trout, including one rainbow that was around sixteen inches long. That's not an especially big fish for the Frying Pan, but it's still a damned nice trout and, honestly, catching *any* trout in the middle of winter still seems slightly unlikely to me. I believe it can be done because I've been doing it off and on for years, and I understand it in theory. But I'm also a mammal, so what makes sense to me are things like big fur coats and hibernation. It will always seem strange to me that a critter can be as cold as a trout on the last day of December and still be alive and well.

After lunch we headed back down to the Roaring Fork, which was now clear of ice, and spent the afternoon fishing that long, riffly pool. There were some midge flies on the water, so we tried midge pupa patterns for a while, first unweighted so they'd drift in the surface film, then with more and more weight to sink them deeper until we snagged bottom and lost our flies. All without a strike.

At one point I saw a single trout rise—the only fish I saw come to the surface on the whole trip—and changed to a dry midge, which I fished for twenty minutes with a growing sense of futility. Then I tried larger caddis pupa, cased caddis, Prince Nymphs, stoneflies, and I forget what all else. Mike changed flies less often, but even he was searching his fly box a little. No pattern turned out to be the silver bullet, but by the time the sun was almost down and the air was cold enough to burn your fingers and make the line ice up in the guides, we'd both landed a couple of trout.

Mike fished like a machine, as he always does. He's the kind of fisherman who seldom agonizes over fly patterns and who can go at it with the same sustained intensity whether he's getting a strike every third cast or three strikes in an eight-hour day.

I have to admit that my own concentration wandered a bit and I got my fish by just going through the motions. Interestingly enough, one approach worked about as well as the other.

That night was New Year's Eve. When we went into the Rainbow Grill for burgers, they were just setting up for the festivities with white tablecloths and linen napkins, but not many revelers had arrived yet. We'd never seen tablecloths and cloth napkins in there before, nor had we ever seen the waiters and waitresses dressed so well. If it were like that all the time, we'd have to find another joint.

It was in the bar there that we heard about Michael Kennedy getting killed when he skied into a tree just up the road at Aspen a few hours earlier. It was big local news, and the prevailing opinion was that he'd asked for it by fooling around on the slopes: skiing without poles while playing an improvised game of football with a mob of other people who, according to one witness, were "running over other skiers." It was an interesting change. Usually the complaints are about snowboarders, or "shredders," as they're called.

As usual, there was a television going over the bar and the newswoman said many people think the Kennedys are "The closest thing America has to a royal family." Someone at the bar was overheard to say, "If you mean a bunch of people who think they're above the rules, yeah, I guess."

The guy looked like a young working stiff; the kind who'd be a fishing guide in the summer and a ski instructor in the winter. Chances are he lived in a trailer sixty miles down the valley because he couldn't afford to pay rent in Aspen. He'd have a 120-mile round trip to work every day, during which he could turn the radio up loud and stew about the wealthy.

When the news moved on to the new catastrophe, Mike turned to me and said, "You know, you and I have taken some pretty stupid chances ourselves over the years."

He was right. Just the night before, Mike, Roy, Art, and I had been sitting in this same bar talking about the old days, which now seem like they were all about pushing too hard and doing things that might have killed us, either right then or eventually. We've slowed down some by now, and compared to some of the stuff we've all pulled, winter fishing seems pretty tame, although it still has that feeling of risk about it that you have to love, if not while you're doing it, then at least later when you're warm and fed. The possibility of something bad happening, say, drowning or hypothermia, is real enough to make you think about what you're doing, even though most days it seems unlikely.

Then again, the worst that could happen always seems unlikely. A few years before, a big sheet of ice had broken loose on the Roaring Fork and slid silently downstream. It knocked a wading fisherman off his feet and pushed him under. He died. Just that quick. It could have happened to any one of us.

Finally Roy raised his glass and said, "Well, at least we're all still on the right side of the grass."

I guess it amounts to a kind of balance. How you live is up to you. Life is *there* to be lived, and no one gets out of it alive. On the other hand, the one thing you don't want carved on your tombstone is, THE DUMB SON OF A BITCH HAD IT COMING.

So Mike and I sat there that night and ate our burgers while the staff hustled and the early drinkers started to drift in. Some of them seemed too loud and wound up too early in the evening. I remembered from my drinking days that even when the whole idea was to roll up your sleeves and get hammered, you still had to pace yourself a little. Another thing you don't want is to be the guy puking in the parking lot while everyone else is still inside having fun.

We'd called Roy earlier and offered to buy him dinner for New Year's, but he said no thanks. He was going to stay up at the cabin, close out the fly shop's business year on the computer, and then maybe go look at the river in the moonlight and have a quiet drink or two. Not that much into partying anymore, he said.

That sounded pretty good: a glass of whiskey down by the river, that illusion of warmth on a bitter night, even though it *is* only an illusion. I don't actually miss drinking anymore, but there are still times when I remember it fondly.

Mike and I finished eating, went back to our motel room, and made fun of a bad horror movie on television. Mike asked, "You think they knew they were making a comedy, or were they really trying to scare us?" We were in bed by ten, having caught our last trout of the old year and planning to get the first of the next in the morning. I remember thinking, Okay, happy new year. May we all stay lucky.